The Berkeley Crisis, 1968

Motel Room, Central California Coast, April 1967

Sausalito, 1968

"All the new thinking is about loss. In this it resembles all the old thinking."

Robert Hass
"Meditations at Lagunitas"
Praise

"Contrary to a widely and firmly held belief, it does not really matter whether the initial image is easy (or something taken to be easy—a genre scene in the style of Vermeer, for example, or a color photograph of an Austrian castle) or difficult (a Jackson Pollock, a Pissarro, or the poor paradox of a blank puzzle). It's not the subject of the picture, or the painter's technique, which makes a puzzle more or less difficult, but the greater or lesser subtlety of the way it has been cut...."

Georges Perec
Life, A User's Manual

"The trouble with great literature is that any asshole can identify with it. "

Peter Handke
The Weight of the World

Irvine Ranch, 1968

Rule Without Exception

Organized by Julia Brown Turrell

T EXCEPTION

Published by the University of New Mexico Press in association with the Des Moines Art Center

Texts

Great Pictures, Mean World
Marvin Heiferman 14

Exactitude and Multiplicity
Paolo Costantini 23

Untitled
Shirley Irons 32

Still Moving
Gus Blaisdell 40

Maryland
Jane Livingston 48

Deeper Into the Country
Mowry Baden 67

San Quentin Point
Mark Haworth-Booth 76

Treatise on the Suppurations of the Industrial World
Bernard Lamarche-Vadel 90

Near Deadline, Nevada
Jeff Kelley 102

Wasteland: A Précis
Olivier Boissière 112

Space begins because we look away from where we are...
Gus Blaisdell 116

A Letter
Michael Schmidt 139

Motel Room, Central California, April 1967 (detail) (p 12)

Great Pictures, Mean World

The sky is blank and the sun comes up bright, nasty, and blinding. It's morning and it's airless, standard weather in Lewis Baltz's photographs. No one grabs a robe reaching for the newspaper on the doorstep. No one takes the dog for a walk. Life is lived indoors, in the shadows. No one goes outside, into the emptiness.

Baltz's barren landscapes are achingly beautiful, like the nineteenth century photographs that surveyed scarred battlegrounds after the dead were removed. Two centuries evidence of a topography of the void: piles of dirt, mounds of rocks, blasts of dust, random fires. American earth, it seems, has always had a story to tell. But for Baltz, the plot's turned ironic; now it's construction that begets destruction.

So, he files eyewitness accounts of building starts and human achievement from the dead zone called success. Things get built, things get sold, things get better; that's how the narrative is supposed to play. But what Baltz absorbs in daylight is darkness. He sees landscape turn into real estate, learns that speculative development turns viral. The garbage in his pictures rises off the ground as profits soar off a page in a bogus business plan.

In such a greedy, overwrought world, even the most basic of building materials take on threatening, mannerist overtones. Sheetrock is bandaged with wall compound. Tentacles of electrical wires flail, ripped from the safety of aluminum conduit. Blank, stucco walls catch light and dirt and would shred

your flesh if you were thrown up against them. Every single, cheaply-made edifice sits on the game board of nature, as seductive—and as perverse—as bonsai.

Clearly, Baltz is attracted to twisted constructs. He's a minimalist burdened with romantic world weariness. In the land of opportunity, curiosity steers him straight toward the epicenters of failure. From Irvine to Maryland to Nevada, from the slopes of Park City to the dumpsite called Candlestick Point, Baltz detects the melodies of the bottom line, and works them up into operas; hundreds of images sing of a country in which humanism and imagination have ceased to be cost-effective.

In fact, Baltz does all he can to make his pictures unlikeable. Prints are tiny, colorless and maddeningly elegant—too smart, and too nasty, to hang over a couch. Sequences are long and so complicated, that they are best read as books. His ambition drives him, like a physicist longing to decode chaos. With deep respect and consternation, Baltz has circled a territory for decades—noting every nuance, systematizing every fact. He's made complex, remarkable, angry pictures. And, any one could detonate like a passive-aggressive; the picture that looks great in your hand might just blow up somewhere inside your head.

Marvin Heiferman
New York 1989

Dana Point 1970 #2

Hidden Valley, Looking Southwest (detail of element #3 from *Nevada*) (p 14/15); *Hidden Valley, Looking South* (element #2 from *Nevada*) (p 16)

Dana Point 1970 #1

Hidden Valley, Looking Southwest (element #3 from *Nevada*) (p 17); *Park City Interior, 10* (element #7 from *Park City*) (p 18/19)

Exactitude and Multiplicity

The entire literary work of Italian author Italo Calvino seems to be concerned with the contrast between human irrationality and nature's "otherness": between changes in society and the immutability of nature, seen as something inexplicable, impassive, ambiguous. For Calvino, the search for a possible relationship of integration and harmony between man and his world is based upon the survival of moral values "on the margin" of current trends, upon an inevitable cohabitation with catastrophe, "as if we had all understood that the end of the world has become our natural habitat, and we could no longer imagine another way to live."

All the writings of Calvino, and especially his latest, *American Lessons* (which Calvino was to have given at Harvard University in 1985-86; each lesson dedicated to one key word: *Lightness, Quickness, Exactitude, Visibility, Multiplicity*, as well as the sixth Lesson, which Calvino was unable to finish, dedicated to *Consistency*; which taken together are meant to describe the specific quality of literature's contribution in the coming millennium) suggest that no body of knowledge exists which warrants a unitarian and global interpretation, but that there exists only "a whirlpool of bits and pieces." It is a world dominated by fatal repetitiveness and immutability, a universal and incomprehensible irrationality, a world in which human reason celebrates ever greater defeats. Calvino challenges the precariousness of "every conceptual systemization" and the emptiness of anthropocentric presumptions, the essential impossibility or futility of making judgements and choices. Instead, he practices "respect for uniqueness" as salvation from "the impossibility of models which claim to be universal and which end up by being universally oppressive." Calvino refutes universal models and unitary interpretations and offers instead an insistent affirmation of limited moments, minute realities; the breakdown of *totality* into *multiplicity*.

Perhaps it is possible to read the entire photographic output of Lewis Baltz in the same manner, as he descends the scale more and more, concentrating heavily on the borders, *on the margin* of an everyday landscape scrutinized for the most minute details, with an obsessive regard for precision.

Baltz seeks to methodically circumscribe the external world but yet establish a relationship. More precisely, he explores an aspect of reality, circumscribed and almost separated from the irrationality of the universal, to which he applies the inquisitive attention of a punctilious observer. We find this same attention given to " things singular," to "the object which is limited and precise" in Signor Palomar—the protagonist who gets his name from a famous telescope—in the most autobiographical of Calvino's books. The reality on which Baltz wants to base awareness is also spotty, disjointed and unstable: "a sprinkling of incongruous phenomena, isolated one from the other, subdivided in their turn by phenomena even more minute."

The complexity of the world resolves itself in a tangle of signs. There remains only the possibility of exercising interrogations and conjectures of "a minute and prolonged attention" upon "the inexhaustible surface" of things. This is an inexhaustible and agnostic exercise, however fleeting, in the face of infinitely interchangeable analyzable objects.

Calvino has demonstrated and practiced two approaches to this "unstable", ungraspable, unknowable *multiplicity*: "the description of things" is practiced continually on their "multiform, inexhaustible surface", with *lightness* and with a taste for mental discipline, for precision and economy of expression; and the cataloguing, or "collectionism" is seen as regularization of the "arbitrariness of existence", as the only logic, however fleeting, like that which regulates the harmonious Japanese gardens, capable of imparting "unity and feelings of homogeneous togetherness to the dispersion of things."

Baltz's photography concentrates on a series of objects saved from dispersion, on a series of images crystallized outside the continuous flow of experience. The photographer-collector ("I think all artists are collectors of images," Walker Evans once said) has here as his responsibility the protection of that which is possible: the representation of differences, of mixtures, of complexities. In the book *Collections of Sand*, Calvino ponders over the glass case of a collection of samples of sand, diverse in color, consistence and provenance, but also in the emotions, sentiments and moods of the collector imprisoned in the glass vial. The writer is enraptured by the minute differences between sand and sand which "demand one's ever changing attention" and lead one little by little to another dimension: "in a world which has no horizons other than these dunes in miniature, where one beach of tiny rose pebbles is never the same as another beach of tiny rose pebbles" and where "every gray is no longer seen as gray once it is broken up into light and dark, shiny and opaque, spherical, polyhydrical and flat granules. Only then do you begin to understand the meaning of gray."

There is lightness in the way we approach a solution, in not aspiring to a definitive globality in our answers, in escaping opaqueness and inertia in order to "fly like Perseus into a different space" and by doing so we illuminate one precise little corner. It is a discreet look, almost a silent one which modifies an unexpected, strategic detail. For Baltz, too, as for Calvino, lightness is associated "with precision and with determination, not with vagueness and the haphazard." The rarefied consistency of Baltz's language grows as a reaction to the heaviness of existence. In a perpetual and never ending pursuit of things and of their opposites, his photographs question that heaviness, densified in the marginal zones, in the waste of a landscape viewed with skepticism, in the emptiness and in the absence of existence.

Laguna Beach, 1969

Exactitude means a well defined design, an incisive image, a language capable of describing with precision the subtleties of the imagination. Exactitude against the "pestilence of language and of images" stripped of inner inevitability, which rapidly fade, leaving a great sense of alienation and discomfort. Baltz starts with the rigorous abstraction of a mathematical notion of space and time, and compares this to the vague, undefined flux of sensations.

Exactitude and lack of definition are the poles between which Baltz's series *Endsites* oscillate. They are indefinite, metaphoric spaces of our contemporary world, possible locations for an architecture of the future, something enigmatic and outside our grasp which do not fit our expectations. All that remains is the possibility of quizzical observation of an immutable and mysterious reality; the *scrutiny* of objects, because "the surface of things is inexhaustible." But this questioning of ever new surfaces also reveals ever new mysteries and continuously reaffirms the frailty of one's knowledge. Baltz, like Ulrich the protagonist in Robert Musil's *The Man Without Qualities*, possesses an incorruptible, deliberate coldbloodedness that goes with exactitude, but apart from and beyond this quality, all is indefinite." And the spaces minutely observed in his photography, always searching for "an infinitesimal fidelity to the multiplicity of reality", are somewhat like ancient pictorial representations of the Japanese "houses-without-a-roof" described by Calvino: "they unveil and at the same time conceal fragments of a secret life."

Paolo Costantini
Venice, Italy 1989

Irvine 1967

San Francisco 1972

THE TRACT HOUSES

16 elements from *The Tract Houses, 1969-1971*

Untitled

Information is identified as a disruption of noise in the brain. A threshold exists which allows noise of a certain magnitude to be interpreted as information. When the noise falls slightly below this threshold, the brain classifies this in an area of uncertainty. This activity takes place in emptiness, in the space in between, which is the synapse. This area of uncertainty is where Baltz's vision rests. This is why it resists categorization.

Unlike work by the Bechers, Dan Graham, or Ed Ruscha, this work mimics the historical romantic photography that celebrated and documented an era of territorial expansion. This was descriptive geography that desired to make the world visible and inspire wonder. "As a peculiar and interesting note of linkage, in 1799 Robert Fulton brought the first diorama to Paris, a large circular view of the New World scenery. It was unpeopled. A theatre for exhibiting this was soon developed, one rule being that it could not include more than 2 human characters. One of the developers of this theatre was Daguerre." (J.B. Jackson, *Landscape as Theatre*; *The Necessity for Ruins*, p 69)

While the organization, tone and clarity of these photographs supposes a traditional view, it is actually a view of landscape as a tamed wilderness, a controlled Other. Is the Other a corporate Other? Is this a Pynchonesque view riddled with paranoia? A national corporate landscape? This is cultural politics rife with conflicted information, under a guise of neutrality presenting information far from neutral, yielding a psychobiological study of culture based on economy.

"Empty history, that is to say, of any teleology except the very abstract one of a general fatalism in which all things run unsteadily to their dissolution." (Jonathan Culler, *Flaubert, the Art of Uncertainty*, p 156).

This cultural criticism inhabits a world seemingly free of illusion, absent of drama. It occupies the space of the margins. What is viewed is fragmentary, traces of the process of building, waste. Everything photographed exists in the space in between. This catalytic synapse defeats a nostalgic vision and our idea of landscape is subverted. We work our way through a series of black windows that perhaps signal painting (a Twombly blackboard, a Moskowitz, an Alex Katz night building) and are rewarded with an entire tract house. We then move through interior details of unfinished walls, dirt floors, wiring askew, to a scattering of activity in the periphery, all couched in the flat language of real estate ads.

A photograph refers to the world and therefore continues to exist beyond its edges. Since it is neither contained nor discreet, the view given is multiplied to create the world. This view unfolds its subtext: The ambiguity of celebrating the future. A relentless style of absence. Feelings are in perpetual transition, the surprise of pleasure is eluded. Have we noted the hostility yet? The difficulty in penetrating those frontal images?

"Losing their names, these things underwent a process of uncreation and reverted to chaos, existing only to themselves in an unstructured world where they were not formally acknowledged, becoming an ever-widening margin of undifferentiated and nameless matter surrounding the outposts of man, who no longer made himself familiar with these things or rendered them authentic in his experience by the gift of naming." (Angela Carter, *Heroes and Villains*)

The flatness with which this politic is presented yields an ironic distancing and an entire discourse with language. The photographs are serial, divided into chapters and punctuated with visual clues. The sequencing calls attention to the structure of communication, sentences which produce a numbness of language. Following one dead vista to another dead end, we experience a loss of innocence with death

as the absolute non-meaning.

We now enter the arena of the elite of the intellect. Irony presupposes dual orders in contrast with one another; appearance vs. reality, the contrast between the apparent and the assumed. This ironic distancing protects the author, but since it contains the possibility of misunderstanding, it exposes as well. When one suspects irony, one becomes an insider privy to the structure, to the intended meaning, satisfying both our desire to participate and to acquire meaning. It is the nature of irony to be unrecoverable. If the author supplies the intent, it is no longer ironic.

In Baltz's work, there is no collusion with the viewer, it is estranged, mute. A flat line on the X axis, revealing nothing but the way light records on film, uncovering nothing of the narrator, concrete in all senses. The implicit irony is arrogant, supported solely by the audience and by the sophistication of photographic technique. This aestheticized detachment is parallel to Flaubert's neutral prose, where the extreme self-consciousness points to the author as it hides him.

"While failure to stimulate does result in inhibition; specific inhibitory neurons in the CNS undoubtedly provide even more precise control" — description of synapse from a handbook of physiology.

Domination requires composure. Control is clearly an issue. This is a pose which invites penetration, as the photographed waste penetrates a wound in the earth. We have to be stimulated by displacement to enjoy this work.

Shirley Irons
New York, 1990

"Irvine: a new Silicon Valley. Electronic factories with no openings to the outside world,

THE NEW INDUSTRIAL PARKS

like integrated circuits. A desert zone, given over to ions and electrons, a supra-human

NEAR IRVINE, CALIFORNIA

place, the product of inhuman decision-making. By a terrible twist of irony it just had to be here, in the hills of Irvine, that they shot *Planet of the Apes.* But, on the lawn, the American squirrels tell us all is well, and that America is kind to animals, to itself, and to the rest of the world, and that in everyone's heart there is a slumbering squirrel. The whole Walt Disney philosophy eats out of your hand with these pretty little sentimental creatures in grey fur coats. For my own part, I believe that behind these smiling eyes there lurks a cold, ferocious beast fearfully stalking us . . . . On the same lawn with the squirrels stands a sign put there by some society or other of Jesus: 'Vietnam, Cambodia, Lebanon, Grenada—We are a violent society in a violent world!"

Jean Baudrillard
America

North Wall Automated Marine International (element #16 from *The New Industrial Parks Near Irvine, California*)
Wall, Rohm Corporation (element #26 from *The New Industrial Parks Near Irvine, California*) (detail) (p 36)

"Baltz's photographs of enigmatic factories fail to tell us anything about them, to recall Brecht's remark about a hypothetical photograph of the Krupp works."

Allen Sekula
Dismantling Modernism

East Wall, Western Carpet Mills (element # 17 from *The New Industrial Parks Near Irvine, California*)

"...the *Tract Houses* through the *Industrial Parks* were Baltz's *Alphaville*, something coming into being..., kind of wonderful in some ways and possibly horrendous in another. This was summed up for me in a remark Baltz made referring to one of the *Industrial Parks* buildings. He said: 'Look at that... you don't know whether they're manufacturing pantyhose or megadeath.' I've quoted that, God knows, a hundred times between then and now....."

Walter Hopps

South Wall, Mazda Motors (element # 40 from *The New Industrial Parks Near Irvine, California*) (detail)

Still Moving

What Follows

Baltz suggested I think about his photography as the remains of lost movies. I still can't. Still, what follows moves from the one to the other—stillness, movement—or between the two.

Coeval

Baltz and Cavell are coeval in my experience. Whenever one of them asks me to write or think the other comes immediately to mind. Four may be intimately involved when two go to bed. Only three are necessary to confuse happily what issues as writing. Can the question of what is mine not arise? Can originality not be stifled if the eyes of one and the voice of the other possess the hand of the third? I am still at it after twenty years. Still—in the future as now and before; still—until and during the present; or some specified time; yet. Still—may what is good remain with you, the spirit still be with you; in spite of what has been said; notwithstanding; nevertheless: but . . . I am still here. Will I still be here? A still as a promise of steadfastness, of enduring returns of the ordinary. I am still here, one who writes from being stuck and being struck. Right now I am struck with my being stuck—not mired, not swamped but with not having a record or an average or a better mastery after twenty years of this intimacy—a threesome, a community at least of my mind. Every time I start I start over. Then so long as I am not dead there would have to have been a before, like now. Still and all. . . . No. Be very still. Be with it still. But how can I sit still for . . . ? This. Which is? At most an unflattering portrait; at worst an exposure, an exhibition of the unoriginal, one inflection of the ordinary prejudiced by the bored. Beginning still.

The last sentence of the "Skeptical Landscapes" section of *Park City* is, "The world depicted here is indeed as Cavell wrote of another, one in which instinct is estranged, birds droop at noon, and strange gods are readied." The other world alluded to is Michelangelo Antonioni's *Eclipse*, in particular the last seven minutes in which places that the lovers once met are returned to repetitively; they are empty; the lovers do not return. I remembered a sprinkler turning in a park, a high one with long arms, the kind they use to water golf courses; and a building under construction, its lower stories covered with straw matting through which ends of the scaffolding protrude; the back of a woman's head, not Vitti's—a signature of vulnerability and the liabilities knowledge is exposed to; an extreme close-up of ants on tree bark, nature autonomous, indifferent; and then the closing shot of the glaring streetlight eclipsing the picture itself. What was significant for Cavell was that these closing moments were not nihilistic. The key to this is his saying that something more happens, the more being the three clauses of his I closed with, letting them eclipse anything more that I might have to say, letting his words still mine—the silence of the pen lifting from the page.

The world of Antonioni and Baltz is a shared one in different media. I wanted Cavell's good words for Baltz's good work and I could find no better words in myself. I still cannot quite find better ones; the best ones I found I discovered long ago, earlier in *The World Viewed* (95-96), a medley follows only slightly improvised: "...his fermata over single shots, which enclose an air of *presentiment*....There is his obsession with the facades of uninhabited, new buildings...; they are not haunted, we know nothing is present inside them, they have no past....Absence is obviously a root topic...; it is registered by the sheen or finish of the frames, which along with the clean, deep lines of perspective, perfects the avoidance of human clutter or arbitrariness; nothing is beyond this space....Male impotence is no longer a personal problem, an ego-alien castration anxiety, but merely a portion of the new human landscape....When love is altogether over, unable even to stir a fantasy of our future redemption, then we have forgone the futurity of our future...(one event is as adventurous or routine as another, one absence or presence as significant or unimportant as another, change as unthinkable as permanence) and to move into that world...."

These are perfect words for Baltz's work; his work perfectly expresses these words, gives these words their perfect expression. Quotations are journeys to origins and their originality lies in having discovered what appositely, definitively they express—each other; all of us; whoever is here. Such company as we still have.

She Wrote There

Epigraph

Kit needed me now more than ever. But something had come between us. I stopped even paying attention to him. Instead, I sat in the car and read a map and spelled out entire sentences with my tongue on the roof of my mouth where nobody could read them.

Sissy Spacek
Holly in Terrence Malick's *Badlands*

In the badlands there is not really any above, not even when the clouds are stacking up—just what you're on and heading towards; always yonder, beyond unreached. They build up out there. Out there above always feels like ahead, the horizon standing straight up in front of you, real washed out most of the time like the huge, empty screen of some gigantic drive-in theatre we can never manage to reach. Nothing on the screen except that bluish white that welding torches give off. Why is the parking lot overgrown with brush, varmints living all around, and none of the speakers on the poles? Why can't we get there? All I want to do is park in that big old passion pit, eat hot buttered popcorn and drink lots of cold cokes, and make out in the back with Kit. Anyway that's what I wanted once, when I thought he was handsomer than anybody I'd ever seen and looked like James Dean.

It's his movie, the one we drive toward, the one we're driving through, leaving the used-up reels in the dust behind us, newspapers with stories about us blowing away—and the soundtrack of it, all we get to know about what's been happening, coming over the radio, interrupting the music. They bring us special bulletins about us! We interrupt this program to bring you...as if they think we need reminding, as if we didn't remember. Kit's movie is behind us and the one they're trying to end with us and them together in it—they want it to end their way; we want it to end ours; but that's justice, I guess—theirs is unrolling up ahead of us, coming toward us, and the interruptions they keep bringing us tell the progress they're making toward bringing both our movies to the same end. But then Kit doesn't think anything really ends. He wonders if he will hear the doctor pronounce him dead; if he will be able to come back and read all about it from the other side; and he wants to die hearing some girl—me—scream his name. Because everything he does he does by first consulting what James Dean would do or look like or say. If James Dean were in a fix like this...? That's his trouble. Kit thinks like a star.

It's getting so that most of the time I don't know where he is, in the car or on the screen or hanging somewhere out there. In between. It's not like that for me since I looked at that stereo picture of the canal bordered on both sides with palm trees, the canal coming to a point but you could feel it going on forever, on and on through the world and out into space like digging that tunnel to China but keeping on digging until you fell through the hole in that Chinese sky, falling forever in outer space like that dead astronaut in *2001*. That stereo photograph reminded me I was just this little girl and that things needn't have unrolled like this even though because of what we've done now this is the only way they could've happened. We have made our headlong way. But they needn't have come out like this. There isn't any other side. The last voice in your ear disappears with you. And you don't return and go to some doctor's or dentist's office or barbershop or newsstand or beauty parlour where there are stacks of newspapers and magazines that tell you how great you were and how famous now you're dead. You go into a hole as dark as that space in *2001* and get covered with dirt and rot.

The countryside we drive through is not the one I see. That landscape is part of Kit's movie. Part of his act is to be real quiet a lot of the time and then come out weird from inside. The part that is really acting is his pretending to think. If I close my eyes or take them off the windshield or side windows, if I look inside I see a landscape that all the color has been drained from, one sort of in black and white, and it shudders and bristles and prickles—is convulsed, erupted, seized like some epileptic, and collapsed, thrashing—but stopped in these movements, held still so long as I'm looking at it; it seems to rush at me, never by me, and it is full of spines and rust and nails and broken wires and glass, crusts of earth broken open even as they collapse—stained with ooze and bristling with sharp spines and hairs and needles. It bristles. Nothing in it moves, everything is fixed once and for all, drained and stained, blacks and white and greys; any sky washed out of its clouds and everything in the landscape exposed in a merciless light. Kit is in a movie he is trying to make end his way. My insides are like a photograph album. Who turns the pages? Why this way? Always silent, never a sound ever in it, the stillness of things arrested: they're falling apart, that's invisible. My mind is a camera and the images rush in, impressing themselves on some wall behind my skull, one that surrounds me, I know because some of the pictures, most of them, recur regularly as nightmares. I can't tell whether the houses are being built or destroyed. Are those basement foundations all that are left? So still, stopped forever, the earth, on it houses, and you can't tell, and nothing in the pictures tells you either, have people been here? left? are they coming back? arriving for the first time? I'd like to see something else, look away. Being with Kit just shoves me deeper into myself, like mine are the nightmare photographs from his movie. He's got room to play. No room for me. I'm stuck. Mine come at me, are inside me before I can do anything, and then never go away. Repulsive. Magnetic. But take pictures inside Kit's head and you'd come out with a James Dean movie that was never made—because it stars Kit; but if he ever was he's not Kit any more. James Dean, Kit's idea of James Dean, is the demon inside and Kit is just the puppet looking up over his shoulder to make sure he's pleasing the demon pulling his strings. Kit can't do anything but pose and James Dean makes sure he does it right because rather than both their reputations being at stake what matters to the demon is that his image be kept pure. He imagines it, works himself into the role, turns toward them and knows he's safe because he's already seen how they are going to take the way he looks—James Dean inside guarantees it. Kit says (James Dean did it) that you gotta live fast, love hard, die young and leave a beautiful memory. I said I was just this little girl.

I copy down in my school notebook as much as I can from the news bulletins. Some guy said, "in what spirit does the girl entrust the narration of her life to the rack of phrases picked from magazine shelves? Which shelves would you recommend? To have company under the sky you will have to entrust its conformation to whichever booth of expression you can occupy." I don't understand the last sentence. I like the way all of it sounds, like risky things can still be alright. At first I thought he was putting us down. But then I guessed he was trying to understand us. Is what it means that while I conformed to Kit, keeping him company, being in his company, in his movie, he conformed only to the empty sky above and straight up in front of us? Is everybody running their own movie? It would be a way of getting out of what isn't inside of you. Kit was always comparing our lives to ordinary, boring ones and saying, "We sure had fun," "It sure was fun," "We had fun, didn't we!" Until I threw in with Kit my idea of fun never included killing.

If Kit knew about the pictures inside me he would try to save me because he still believes he loves me. He'd hold me down like that kid at school who had epileptic fits. "Somebody hold her. Get her mouth open. Put a spoon or pencil on her tongue. If she swallows it she'll choke to death." When I think of that kid thrashing and foaming and strangling I always picture that little soft flesh that hangs at the back of my mouth and I imagine it ringing like the crazy clappers on a doorbell or alarm clock. It's weird to think you have a roof inside your mouth and under the top of your head. Since we burned my daddy's house down the only roof I've had over my head is the car's. That roof over my head and beyond that the badlands. But with the roof of my mouth what seems to be outside or above of it is me, thinking. If I could look down inside I would see that roof. I also feel I am above the top of my head: I'd look down through the top of my skull, through the brain case, and on down through the roof of my mouth, my thought falling onto my tongue, waiting there to see if I was going to speak it or swallow it. It might fall

in all at once, the roof, like dreams collapse, leaving just the walls and screen around the drive-in. Empty screen, headless speaker poles, and the lot overgrown with tumbleweed and briars and thistles.

I saw a weird movie when I was in detention. It was about these two girls from Texas. One of them was so like me that I thought I really had finally managed to get free of Kit and into my own movie. She was "always the fallin' one," her very old mother said; off beds and finally off a balcony into a swimming pool full of paintings of Creatures-from-the-Black-Lagoon-type monsters. She fell right into the pregnant belly of the female one which was being strangled by the male one. The broken water

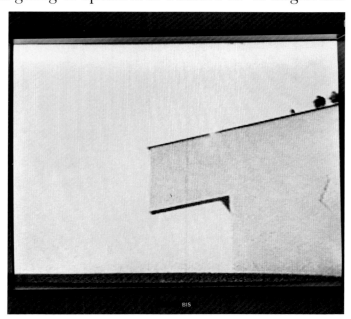

made the creatures come to life. They flowed and writhed. Their tongues stuck out, curled up, vibrated like rattles on a snake, and their dangling penises swayed back and forth underwater. She was saved by the silent, pregnant artist who put the murals in the bottom of the pool.

Some months after momma died daddy took me to Mac's barbershop. He told Mac to shave my head. Mac refused. But he and daddy were lifetime friends—they hunted and fished together and drank beer—and so he finally gave in to daddy's wishes and did it. Daddy's idea was that this would somehow stop my growth which with momma dead was more than he could handle. I held my head high and bit my lower lip. I looked out of the corners of my eyes, my head held real still, so still I thought my concentration and shame and anger would make it shake as bad as that epileptic kid. But it didn't and I watched my curls and tresses and locks fall on the shiny linoleum and down the front of the smock Mac tied around my neck, and onto my shoulders. As Mac brushed me off and blew the itchy hair off my neck and shoulders the door to the back room opened and the huge black janitor from school came out with his pushbroom. I noticed a little window of one-way glass in the door. He had a huge bare head, his body was hairless and he always wore bib overalls without a shirt. He was scary and the girls at school all said he never wore anything underneath his overalls. At school, at the end of the day, he cleaned all the blackboards and chalk trays with underwear—ladies' slips and men's and women's underpants. He had a bagful and he'd dip them in his watering can and wipe all the English and math lessons off the blackboards.

Now here he came with his pushbroom to sweep away all my fallen hair. I can still see the thick black bristles of his broom as they pushed my hair toward the backroom. Where did he get all that old underwear? Why not plain old rags? Is this what daddy wanted? But he didn't see the bristles of the pushbroom. Why didn't he have Mac shave me everywhere, even under the arms so I'd end up like an undressed Barbie doll. Now my hair was part of the janitor's collection. Behind the one-way glass slot in that door I imagined the janitor was building some voodoo woman out of stuff from the floor of the barbershop and out of the trash and garbage cans in the alleys all over town. If daddy had had Mac shave me all over I could've been the janitor's albino daughter.

Everything was dead still while Mac shaved me. None of the men looked up from their girlie or true crime magazines. They hung their heads like they were ashamed. With the magazines open and their heads hung down they looked like depressed animals staring stupidly into their feed troughs. A boy from school was getting a facial when I came in, Mac covering his face with a hot towel, then removing it and squeezing the kid's zits and blackheads. When he agreed to do what daddy wanted he covered the boy's face and left him that way all the time I was in the chair. The kid's snuffling nose was all of his face that showed.

Everything in the barbershop was shiny—the floor, the pinups on the walls, the city league trophies, and the mirrors you looked into as you got smaller and smaller, but never disappearing, always down there somewhere, no matter how small, going on forever but not like the dead spaceman in *2001* because you were always here, sitting there. Every time I hear that music I see that corpse in a space suit falling through blackness. And the shelves with the combs and scissors and straight razors and brushes were mirrors too. So they caught and held the things in their own images and fixed them in their own reflections, made them like conceited and stuck up and weird and

powerful—the razors and scissors more threatening than usual because their reflections gave them ideas about themselves; what they looked like. Their images wrapped around them like cocoons. I wondered what it would be like to have my own reflection wrap around me. I saw it go in and go out like a soul in a movie. With my head shaved I looked like one of those pictures of what the villagers did to women who slept with the enemy. I saw in my mind that girl in the movie locked in her parents' cellar until her hair grew out and they would not be constantly reminded of the disgrace she brought on them. Her only visitor was a black cat. I see her licking the saltpeter off the walls of the cellar just like she licked the blood of her dying boyfriend's mouth. And scratching her fingernails down the walls till her fingers bleed. Saltpeter and her memories and the black cat and blood are all that keep her from going insane down there. My shaved head made me real aware of all the hairy parts I still had. Instead of humiliating me, daddy set me apart and made me different. People stared. That was the real beginning of my movie.

for Patricia McDonald
Gus Blaisdell
Albuquerque, 1990

MARYLAND

A peculiar problem resulting from Lewis Baltz's approach is that the subject, treated as much for the artist's view to its abstract, planar qualities as with concern for its meaning or even its "nature," may carry no transcendent spirit. We automatically look for emotionally and morally evocative qualities in photography in a way we don't in painting or sculpture.

The striking conclusion one comes to in considering the Maryland photographs is that Baltz attains a penetrating psychological layer of content not by acceding to a more atmospheric look than before, but on the contrary by concerning himself more strictly than ever with factualness—and thereby virtually de-estheticizing the work. In many of the Industrial Park photographs one sensed a fleeting atmospheric flavor and an underlying "message" about the cheap edifices of our time. But even at their most poignant, the works remained finally obdurate. The emotionally stimulative attributes in Baltz's work are like the presence of ghosts. The photographs do not yield to romanticization; still they are increasingly establishing their authority as much more than formal exercises. It is important to acknowledge the historical conventions behind these photographs, locatable not just in photography but in the painting of Mondrian and in Bauhaus design principles. Yet the presiding importance of the photographs may have little to do with this: they really are records of particular places in a particular time. In this Baltz recalls August Sander, though his compositional instincts are nearer to the Americans, Sheeler, Siskind and Evans. It cannot be escaped that in comparison to his precursors he projects a slightly cold mentality. The chill of the pictures is part of their gradually riveting fascination for us.

To enumerate the various departures from photographic convention that one can find in examining the work closely is beyond the scope of the present format. It is however irresistible to mention a particularly haunting feature of Baltz's photographs, noticeable especially in the present ones: light in these works appears not to equate with luminosity but merely to serve textural and compo-

sitional definition. In other words, light doesn't appear to us as establishing time of day or any mood at all; instead its ability to visually condition plain things—both "purely formal" and "purely factual"—is explored. Surfaces and compositional juxtapositions meet light halfway; the vector is elusive.

One didn't exactly think about it beforehand, but when it turned out some days after Baltz's arrival in Washington that he was photographing in suburban Maryland—in Wheaton, Silver Spring, Bethesda, Chevy Chase, Towson and College Park—it made perfect sense in the light of his past photographs. The outlying residential areas are a side of "The Capital" that has a special character, and a character that is important in understanding the vastly more familiar central city. The truth about the suburbs bears little relation to the popular image of them as more or less uniformly affluent reaches of housing for the families of the powerful. What Baltz has chosen to record are unintentionally eccentric lower middle-class structures, recently built, and the accidental-seeming peripheral landscape patches surrounding them. The specific examples of architecture that Baltz photographs will be interesting to future historians from a sheerly documentary viewpoint. The industrial buildings and mass produced suburban houses of the 1970's may actually be attributable to the very year by twenty first century

Maryland 8, 1976; Maryland 14, 1976 (detail) (pp 46/47); *Maryland 2, 1976* (detail) (pp 48/49)

scholars based on "stylistic" (mostly economy-determined) features that we take for granted and barely notice. Moreover these buildings will doubtless need to be examined photographically, since the chances are slight of their enduring physically for more than a few decades. The Maryland series represents a significant departure for the artist. Baltz has said that he attempted more scrupulously than ever to eliminate atmospheric overtones—"I hope that these photographs are sterile, that there's no emotional content". With the Maryland photographs, in contrast to the Tract Houses or the Industrial Parks, he deliberately tried to concern himself with, in his words, information clues: "I wanted to tell something about the place". Perhaps the most obvious schematic departure evident in these pictures is their asymmetry. Something bordering on chaos begins to occur and yet an unexpected thing happens: new symmetries or schemes assert themselves, more sophisticated and complicated interrelationships of parts of each picture. The works are not disorderly; rather they are ordered with greater complexity than before. The most elementary example of the shift away from frontality is seen in *Maryland 8*, which is almost a parody on his own past work, taking precisely the kind of subject we've come to associate with Baltz and simply changing the angle from which it is shot. In *Maryland 12*, however, we see the full

measure of his willingness to get inside his subject and to work with increasingly elaborate systems. This photograph has a special kind of symmetry along a vertical axis; it is as though architecture and landscape are exact counterparts and even equivalents. The Maryland photographs break not only from Baltz's own precedent but from certain accepted rules of photography. Finesse of detail is sacrificed for a steely, impenetrable effect. The skies, for instance, are bleached; and foreground detail is often obscured in featureless shadow. In fact subtleties of feature in general are all but disregarded as a means to establish internal richness; this is in distinct contrast to the earlier work.

These subtly licentious techniques work to the advantage of the photographs. The more one studies them, the more one recognizes a completely original sensibility. As Baltz year by year becomes more experienced, he gradually drains out of the photographs their schooled quality, their overtone of contrivance and calculation. From the beginning he has taken only two or three basic ideas and laboriously, continually refined them, reaching the point at which he can make startling departures. It is worth adding that in *Maryland 25* Baltz has made one nod to a sort of super reductive image. It provides a glimpse into the artist's hidden side (he is so consistently disciplined and systematic)—for this work is quite undeniably a conscious joke.

Jane Livingston
Washington, D.C., 1976

Venice 1972

2000 Strong's Drive, Venice, California, 1972

Fluorescent Tube (element #4 from Nevada) 1977 (pp 56/57)

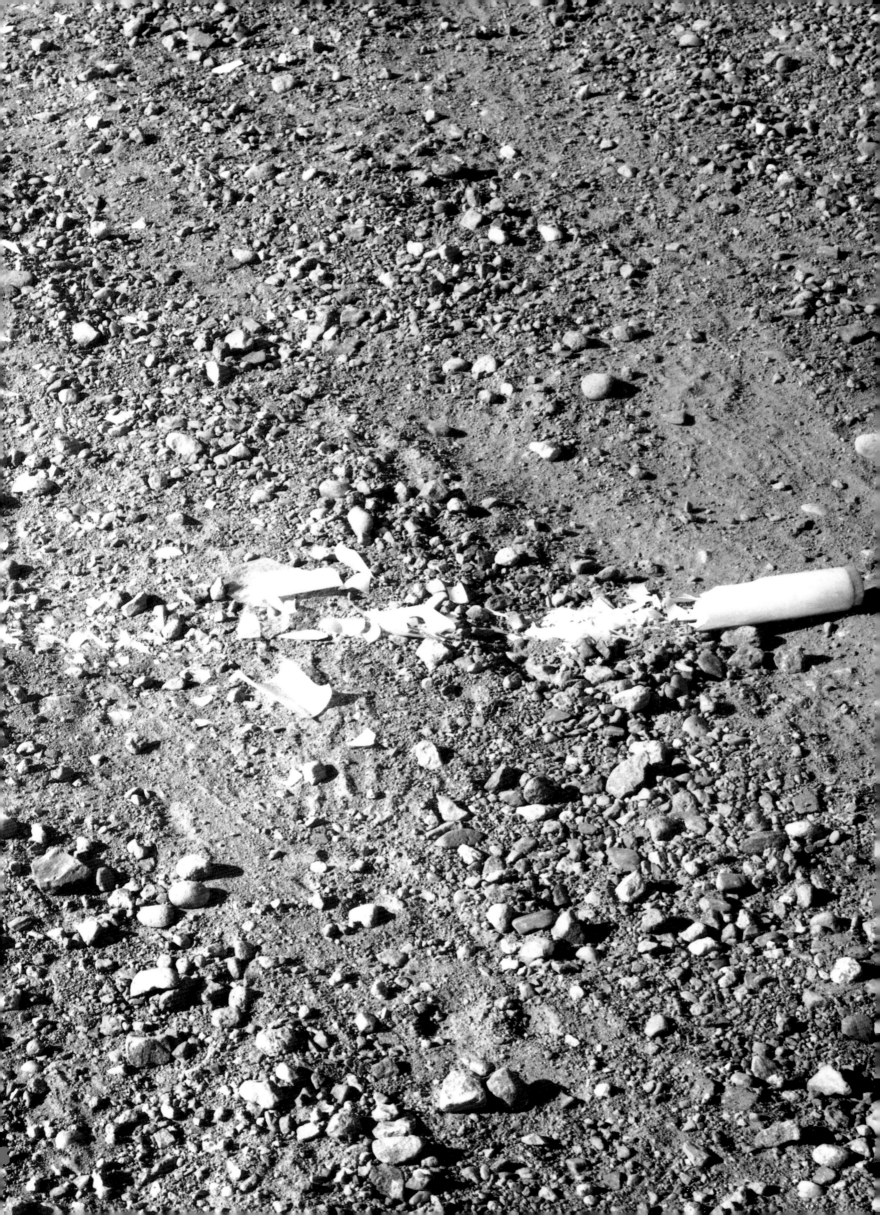

NEVADA

Mustang Bridge Exit, I-80 (element #15 from *Nevada*) 1977
Model Home, Shadow Mountain (element #8 from *Nevada*) 1977 (detail) (p 58)

Night Construction, Reno (element #7 from *Nevada*) 1977

Lemon Valley, Looking Northwest, Toward Stead (element #13 from *Nevada*) 1977

Lemon Valley, Looking Northeast (element #2 from *Nevada*) 1977

PARK CITY

Deeper Into the Country

On a summer day in 1984 I took Lewis Baltz to the Heartland Avenue dump outside Victoria. Like most waste-management facilities, this landfill is a strange and unnerving place. The most frightening aspect is its physical instability. The ground is hard-surfaced, but springy. The feeling is like walking on a vast, crusted mattress. Even while standing still, you can feel the land vibrate like jello when the heavy trucks go by.

Baltz took many photographs that day, and I watched him move around the site, stopping occasionally to take a picture, usually of something he'd found at his feet.

What impressed me was his bodily investigation of the place, a padding, nosing kind of inspection—purposeful and hesitant at the same time.

Park City

I wonder about the impulse to build out in the so-called wilds. And I wonder about building on (or near) contaminated ground. Since I'm guilty of it myself (I live a mile from the Heartland Avenue dump) it's a subject that comes around again and again. We test our well water periodically and close our windows against the stench of the landfill when the wind sets the "wrong" way. The question is more perplexing when the home that's built is a "second" one, and this I gather is what we see at Park City — substantial homes built for bourgeois clients whose primary address is in Salt Lake City. In 1981 Lewis Baltz published a book of photographs he'd taken at Park City from 1978 to 1980.

In only one instance, roughly half-way through the *Park City* volume, do I see a photograph with people. Three guys in the shot, obviously workers taking a break from the construction site. The day must be warm. All three wear T-shirts. The shot is like a Rosetta Stone for much of what precedes and all of what follows.

If you look at the book from the point of view of a builder, you can experience the photographs in a physical way, giving every page a padding, nosing kind of inspection, purposeful and hesitant at the same time. The book provokes reveries about the processes involved in site preparation, form construction, foundation pour, framing, roofing, drywall and finish.

Now and then something's out of place, like Plate 3 (*Between West Sidewinder Drive and State Highway 248, looking West*) where an imported pile of black soil poses beside an old foundation, poured God knows how long ago. Similarly, the concrete work in the middle of Plate 5 looks like foundations for another rancher-style place like the building in the far right middle ground. A closer look and you change your mind. The pour is old, non-residential, and probably used to support industrial gear at one time. I got all the way to Plate 14 (*Prospector Village, Lot 85, looking West*) before I began to get a glimpse of contemporary building practice. The site is complicated with evidence of tailings and debris from earlier mining activity.

One of the ongoing concerns of the contractor on a building site is clean-up. It appears under "site control" on most building estimates. The conditions at Park City must have posed real problems in this area. How, for example, was the backhoe operator to know which pile of debris to remove? The one with stud ends, aspenite cut-offs, five eighths and G decking plywood, tar paper and soil? Or the one with concrete fragments, corrugated sheet metal, checked timber, cable and soil? So, by the time I reach the middle of the book, I'm persuaded that one of Baltz's preoccupations is with layered cultural material, each layer imbedded in local soils and redolent with the building practice particular to the time.

Prospector Park, Subdivision Phase III, Lot 160, looking West (element #54 from *Park City*) (detail)

Looking Northeast from Masonic Hill (element #2 from *Park City*) 1980 (pp 64/65)

An archaeologist would deplore Baltz's technique. There doesn't seem to be any system, any path or conspicuous sequence. Even if Baltz had ordered these piles of rubble according to an unfathomable system, think what the dozer will do to them when they reach the landfill.

Scale

Some of this dirt and debris will go back in place, a process that's already begun in Plate 57 (*Snowflower Condominiums, looking Southwest towards Three Kings and Clementine Lifts*). You can see that after the foundation was poured, the backhoe operator came back to the site and dumped piles of earth along the inside of the wall. These will reinforce the wall and prevent collapse when the building is back-filled around its perimeter later on. Plate 57 is an interesting picture because it introduces a miniaturized field. The hillside has been swathed into ski runs and this rudimentary landscaping gives a sensation of smallness. If you run back through the book, you won't find another picture that so effectively reduces the size of the mountains. This picture is a central one as well. It seems like a set-up for what's to follow, an inspection of contemporary building practice with particular attention to the debris that accumulates around that practice. Heaps of paint-trays, mud pans, drywall fragments, encrusted tape compound, insulation and wood chips fill the foregrounds of these pictures and reduce the rooms to doll-house scale. Again, I can imagine Baltz nosing around these rooms, his attention fixed on the floor.

Improbable scale shifts occur from time to time when Baltz focuses on a "feature." I'm thinking of the mammoth field-stone fireplace in Plate 85 (*Park City interior, #24*). This rustic honey bulges out of the wall, fossil—encrusted and topped with the obligatory roughhewn wooden mantle. The surrounding space shrivels.

Snowflower Condominiums, looking Southeast toward Three Kings and Clementine Lifts (element #57 from *Park City*) 1980

And in a remarkable photograph, (*Park City interior, #33*) Plate 94, a similar scale inversion occurs because he's shot the room after the paint contractor has blown on the texture but before the paint's been applied. The room dwindles behind a hail of cottage cheese.

Back in 1971 Baltz made some remarkable photographs of tract houses in Southern California. In the light of Park City, they are prototypal. Most are shot with relentless regard for the integrity of the picture-plane. But there are a couple of them that are cranked around to a three-quarter view (in each case a view of an entire two story building). Because the camera angle is high for *Tract House #4*, the whole structure resembles a doll house. Stucco-streaked windows clinch the impression. We are looking at a diminutive *idea* of a house, not the real thing.

Building practice and scale go hand in hand, whether I'm looking at traces of by-gone mining site construction or looking at contemporary domestic building habits revealed by the debris accumulating and mingling as the structures near completion. It's a wonderful way to lead the viewer back and forth from particularity to generalization. I can look at these pictures through the eyes of a builder/archaeologist and relive the processes as though they were occurring in real time, or I can look at them through the eyes of a photographer who's preoccupied with scale and who can therefore compress or expand the objects and their field to the point where consciousness must supply an arbitrary time-line. As soon as that happens, an unreal or unworldly atmosphere invades the work, and the viewer is set free to speculate and invent meaning.

Between West Sidewinder Drive and State Highway 248, looking Southwest (element #6 from *Park City*) 1980; *Between West Sidewinder Drive and State Highway 248, looking West,* and *Prospector Village, Lot 85, looking West* (elements #5 and #14 from *Park City*) 1980

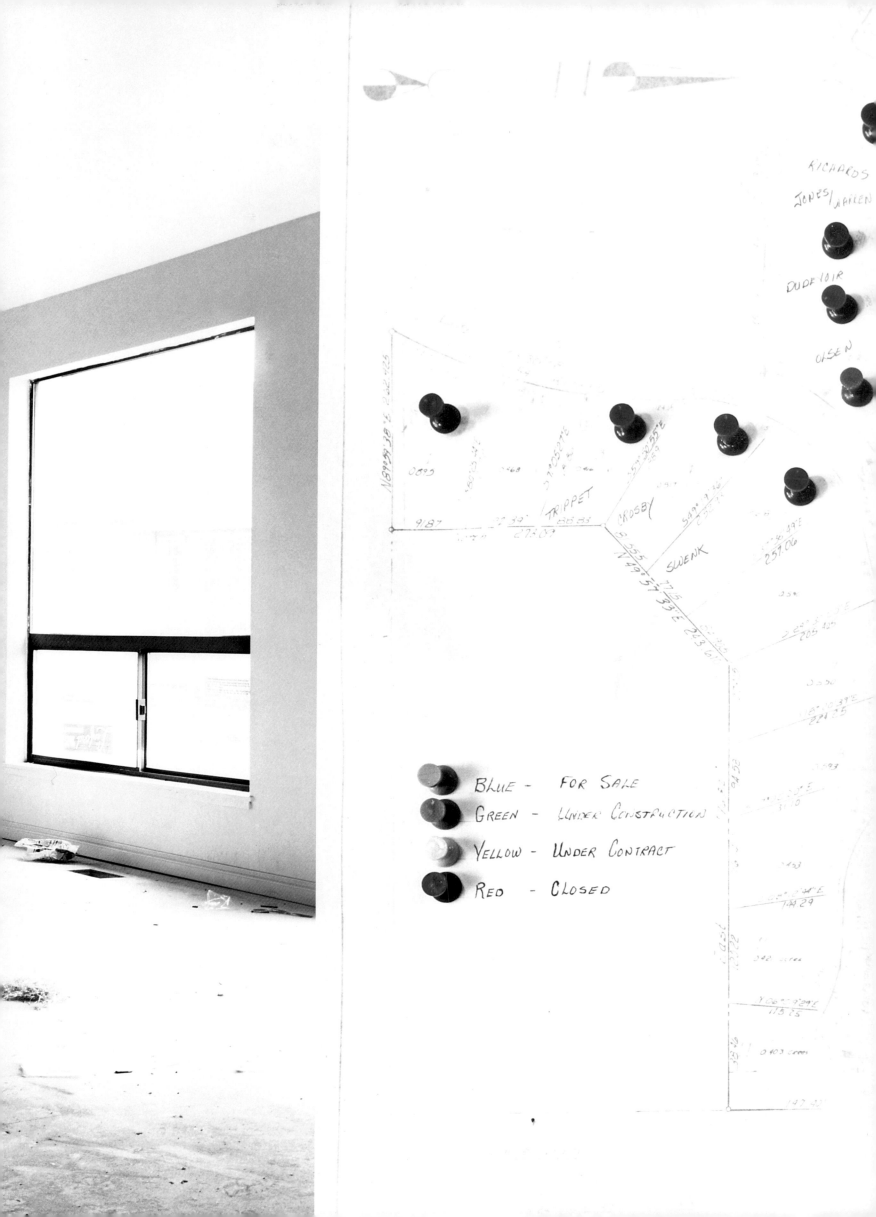

Deeper in the Country

I'm still no closer to an answer to the question I asked earlier. Why indeed do we have this impulse to build homes out in the so-called wilds? Quite apart from the pleasure of hearing coyotes late at night when you are warm in your bedroom or watching a doe walk across your lawn in the morning, there is an issue of class and identity.

I wonder if the bourgeois struggle for identity depicted in many French paintings of the late 19th century couldn't be found again in Lewis Baltz's *Park City*. T.J. Clark says, in *The Painting of Modern Life*, "To call someone vulgar is to say he insists on a status which is not yet proved or well understood by him, not yet possessed as a matter of form. It is a damaging charge, made by one bourgeois against another. To have access to Nature be the test of class is to shift the arguement to usefully irrefutable ground: the bourgeoisie's Nature is not unlike the aristocracy's Blood: what the false bourgeois has is false nature, nature *en toc*, *la nature des environs de Paris*; and beyond or behind it there must be a real one, which remains in the hands of the real bourgeoisie." (p 156)

Mowry Baden
Victoria, B.C., 1990

Park City Interior #24 (element #85 from *Park City*) 1980; *Park City Interior #39 and Park City Interior #41*
(elements #100 and 102 from *Park City*) 1980 (p 70/71); *Park City Interior #24* (element #85 from *Park City*) 1980 (p 72)

SAN QUENTIN POINT

"It might be more useful, if not necessarily more true, to think of photography as a narrow, deep area between the novel and film."

This set of photographs illuminates a variety of questions, including the remark quoted previously from a recent essay by their maker, Lewis Baltz.[1] *San Quentin Point* is akin to a magnetic field. The photographs, considered as a totality, re-order several trains of thought, adjust a number of elements of photographic history, provoke redefinitions of the medium in which they were made and—to this reader/viewer—possess an unusually acute personal resonance. Like all substantial works of art *San Quentin Point* realigns surrounding phenomena and establishes a new symbolic landscape.

San Quentin Point was photographed in 1982-1983 and occupies a special position in the evolution of the photographer's work. The American photographic tradition relevant to Lewis Baltz is intricate but well defined. In 1915 Charles Sheeler photographed *Bucks County Barn* flat-on, close-up, in detail and with artistry. His example as a modernist in photography and painting was influential in the following decades. Walker Evans photographed small-town facades with a similar plain-spoken subtlety in the 1930's. More crucially for Baltz, Frederick Sommer brought to American photography important ingredients of European Surrealism, which he fused with a technique learned from Edward Weston. Sommer's Arizona landscapes were published in *VVV*, the magazine of New York Surrealism, at the instance of Max Ernst in 1944: these photographs proposed that the desert landscape was not a setting for anthropomorphic display but a site indifferent to human concerns, and almost lunar in aspect. Sommer also introduced into American photography an iconography of the disregarded—or "unphotographable"—such as visceral organic details and industrial detritus. Baltz's later concerns seem to be accurately indicated by Sommer's view of the photograph: not a "moment of truth, but as truth before the fact." The importance of Sommer in relation to the photographers associated by the term "New Topographics" is stated with exemplary clarity by Jonathan Green in *American Photography: A Critical History 1945 to the Present* (1984). Lewis Baltz has illuminated, by his practice, some of his distinguished elder colleague's most inaccessible work. Baltz's first book, *The New Industrial Parks Near Irvine, California* (1975), is a foundation block of "New Topographics" ideology. It is informed by detachment, irony and allusiveness. The photographs superimposed on the subjects visual ideas drawn from Minimal Art, a genre whose unadorned structures sometimes themselves achieved the dimensions of garages or hi-tech workshops. The underlying theme of the series is the proposition not simply that

such buildings resemble works of art but that the constructions of the socio-economic order are precisely that. The world, like it or not, as "installation," asking what is installed, by whom and how? *Nevada* (1978) records New West urbanization. Here the thematic includes a set of contrasts featuring artificial and natural light, the latter presented as ebbing into twilight. *Park City* (1980) is a series of 102 photographs which describe the construction of the ski-resort of this name a few miles east of Salt Lake City, Utah. Bearing on the extensive nature of this project is Baltz's long-standing awareness of the dubious veracity of the single photography. In his text for *Park City* Gus Blaisdell developed the notion of "Landscape-as-Real-Estate." Baltz's photographs of Park City reflect his decision that such places are most interesting, or revealing of themselves, at the moment when their construction is incomplete. Part of his point may be that these places are, from a certain point of view, intrinsically unfinished. If this is correct, Baltz's position chimes accurately with that of Joan Didion in her essay "Many Mansions" (1977), reprinted in *The White Album* (1979).

Here Didion reflects on the specific qualities and symbolic properties of "the new official residence for governors of California, unlandscaped, unfurnished, and unoccupied since the construction stopped in 1975." The implications of this eloquent shell lead her to conclude: "I have seldom seen a house so evocative of the unspeakable." Similarly, the notion of the building plot as site of mythic identity, and its use as a central metaphor, is found not only in *Park City* but in *Paris, Texas.* In the Wim Wenders/Sam Shepard film a colour snapshot of a barren plot provokes a child's question to his father: "Why would you want to buy a vacant lot in Paris, Texas?" And the reply: "I forgot." Baltz was to turn next to a typical landscape of forgotten things.

San Quentin Point, photographed four and five years after *Park City* began, is an example of the genre Lewis Baltz has evolved, which we might call the oblique epic even if that is a contradiction in terms. The present writer first saw the *San Quentin Point* photographs in the form of a slide presentation given by Lewis Baltz at an international gathering held in Graz, Austria, in the autumn of 1983. The experience emphasized two points. First, that these photographs occupy an ambiguous position as regards the sense of scale. Given the camouflage afforded by context, some photographs in the series could easily pass as, on the one hand, photo-electron microscope enlargements, and, on the other hand, reductions from enormous extra-terrestrial images: say, the structure of an albumen print in extra close-up or, conversely, the Badlands from space. Second, an international audience found a great deal to look at in these photographs. I recall that Baltz remarked on that occasion that "it is probably not necessary to know this but San Quentin Point is adjacent to the most notoriously affluent and bourgeois suburban county in California." Apparently the equally notorious prison at San Quentin withheld the speculating arm for many years, but at last luxury apartment blocks, boutiques and parking lots prevailed. A further point I recall from that memorable first viewing of *San Quentin Point*: "I was curious to see if I could photograph near where I live," Baltz said. At the time I found this remark surprising. I now find it revealing. The audience in Graz was able, I think, first to perceive *San Quentin Point* in international aesthetic terms; second, to respond to its subject as somehow a common property. The "Waste Land" at *San Quentin Point* touched a nerve. The work evoked a complex iconography of the late 20th century and aroused simultaneously a private psychological fascination.

I have in front of me my immediate impressions of *San Quentin Point*: "We saw pictures of the rank vegetation characteristic of bombsites and railyards. Bedsprings or whatnot, cloth pressed into the earth as if steam-ironed, thistles spraying up regardless, nameless slimy things, rendered with the exquisiteness with which any trash can, quoth Walter Benjamin in days of yore, could and would be beautified by photography....As honesty, a dilapidated, beautiful and plentiful plant, which may be known by another name in America, flourishes especially beside English motorways, sturdy common things glinted among the bits of broken glass and broken most things at San Quentin Point. They gained stature as they multiplied...."[2]

Later I heard someone asking about the role of the photographer and Baltz spoke of how a photographer could, maybe, roam the world assigning values: "But this robs the viewer of participation in the work. It robs viewers of the responsibility they must have." Working in sequences, sometimes extensive ones, is a way of setting up a field or screen on which the viewer can—or has little choice other than to—project some perhaps hitherto invisible messages more or less in private as well as at some length.

San Quentin Point struck a contemporary note with the present writer at Graz because the photographs seemed to be the work of someone who, like his audience, lived in a world familiar with an extra-terrestrial perspective on itself. His photographs seemed to imply the imagery of extreme distance, but also—as I have said—of the extreme close-up. They are part of a peculiarly modern visual field. His use of the camera is also part of the sensibility of this time. For some years I have been intrigued by the fact that the modern detective emerges in the same decades as the professional photographer. The fascination is compounded by the participation of the major English language novelist of that period, Charles Dickens, in the formulation of the fictional detective. Dickens conferred on his "Inspector Bucket" in *Bleak House* a kind of functional or forensic vision which is actually, like his own actual vision and his literary style, highly photographic. Photography has always had forensic objectivity as one of its main options or, depending on the motives of the photographer, disfigurements. The characteristic photographs of Diane Arbus and Garry Winogrand accept and accentuate the forensic capability of the medium. They present phenomena untrammeled by emotion or empathy. Their photographs are near-mugshots or surrogate "scenes of the crime" in which we look principally for clues.[3] This forensic stance is characteristic of Baltz's method. Part of the iconography of this kind of photography is to be found in Walter Benjamin's famous essay: "Not for nothing have Atget's

photographs been likened to those of the scene of a crime. But is not every square inch of our cities the scene of a crime? Every passer-by a culprit? It is not the task of the photographer—descendant of the augurs and haruspices—to reveal guilt and point out the guilty in his pictures?" Perhaps *San Quentin Point* has—as mediated by these photographs—become an arena where such a social investigation can be enacted. The photographs follow, as I believe, the tendency of Walter Benjamin's illuminating remarks. Nearer at hand these photographs are also made yet more transparent by two remarks from the great cinematographer Nestor Almendros. He comments first on photography as transformation: "Through the lens, something like an automatic transfiguration is produced on the photographic emulsion. Everything seems more interesting on film than in life." Secondly, on the frame: "By means of the camera's viewfinder, the outside world goes through a process of selection and organization. Things become pertinent; thanks to the parameters of the frame, they take shape in relation to vertical and horizontal limits. We know at once what is good and what is bad. Like the microscope, the frame is an analyzing tool."[4]

These remarks help to account for the most unexpected fascination of *San Quentin Point*. Lewis Baltz has, in the guise of a forensically neutral statement, actually beautified the phenomena of an urban waste land. Secondly, by using the frame as a microscope he has suggested that the disturbances

observed here in miniature are legible as part of a larger allegory. He observes a set of violations set in a microcosm and, to this viewer, the photographs resonate with an irony reminiscent of the manner in which the behavior of Lilliputians was chronicled by Jonathan Swift.

Finally, I find that, as was hinted in my opening remarks, the choice of San Quentin Point as a subject is a peculiarly evocative one. It seems that waste ground is part of the natural adoptive territory of puberty/early adolescence—a disregarded tract profusely littered with fragments and oddments of the adult world, with the exception of adults themselves. Here parts of the made world are found in mysterious bits, unmanufactured by time and use. Animal, vegetable and mineral phenomena form strange and unintentional constellations. At a certain age many children wander among the luxuriant unplanted thickets of such places. They engender afterwards a surprising intensity of recall. It is unlikely that anyone could be sentimental about such places—or ever quite unlock their hold on a distant strata of the imagination. It is surprising and somewhat shocking to find such a primal and ambiguous world exposed in these photographs of San Quentin Point. It is an experience we may feel more likely to encounter in either a novel or a film but have been taught by some few photographers to find elsewhere too.

Lewis Baltz has recently imposed a degree of finality on his work of the past dozen years. He regards *San Quentin Point* as the third and final portion of a trilogy which began with *The New Industrial Parks Near Irvine, California* and continued with *Park City*. (In this scheme of things, the notable series on Nevada is placed by its author in a perhaps unnecessarily modest position as "experiment".) The idea of the trilogy changes the way we might read each of the three parts which make up the larger whole. Clearly there is a progression—or should we merely say an alteration—from the almost dapper formal specimens scrutinized in *The New Industrial Parks Near Irvine, California*, to the theatre of order and chaos assembled in *Park City*. In this volume, the third term of the "Industrial" trilogy, it appears that chaos has claimed total victory to the point that even the notion of "victory"—by what and over whom?—is displaced from the usual map of meanings. The photographs seem to utter only a sharp entropic decline and the final images resemble very little at all that one can make sense about.

That is one view of the trilogy. There is another possibility. In the opinion of the photographer the last photograph in *San Quentin Point* is as highly ordered—or even *more* highly ordered—than the first images in *The New Industrial Parks Near Irvine, California*. How can this be? To describe what kind of order is the subject of these last photographs it is probably most convenient to reach into the vocabulary of political science. The analogy or metaphor is with that kind of Anarchy which is not chaos but rather a form of non-hierarchical social organization so complexly ordered as to defy the sort of analysis useful in describing dictatorships, democracies, and so on. That metaphor has the virtue of inviting the visitor to circle the contents of the book, and each image in it, with the new sense of what order might be and how the evidence for it might be found.

Mark Haworth-Booth

London, 1986

Notes

1   Lewis Baltz, "La mission photographique de la DATAR: A Critical Appreciation."

2   These notes form part of my essay "A Letter from Graz" published in *Aperture No. 90* (1983). Lewis Baltz's text from Graz is published in *Camera-Austria No. 11/12* (1983).

3   These notions are advanced in my essay "A Connoisseur of the Art of Photography in the 1850's: The Rev. C.H. Townshend," *New Mexico Studies in the Fine Arts, Volume IX*, 1984, The Beaumont Newhall Lectures, pp 14-15.

4   See Nestor Almendros, *A Man with a Camera*, London 1985, pp 10, 12-13.

Treatise on the Suppurations of the Industrial World

Is that known in the United States? That after the generation which culminates with the likes of Robert Frank and Lee Friedlander, the name and work of Lewis Baltz have become in Europe the object of the greatest interest in circles specifically concerned with photography? No other name, no other body of work from the United States has sustained such favorable consideration, has been surrounded by such enthusiasm and respect.

The artist's discretion and the rigor of his work certainly have quite a bit to do with it. But even more so, Lewis Baltz's name symbolizes for us Europeans simultaneously the highest degree of conscience of a typically American artistic heritage, as well as an act of rebellion which finds a sounding board in our own culture, where the strategy of dissensus is the first significant mark of any innovative enterprise. For such is the mode of appropriation that we favor concerning works of the mind, be it among ourselves, within the Common Market countries, or from America.

A body of work must overturn, or at least substantially subvert, the legal prescriptions in force prior to its elaboration, prescriptions which dictate what a work of modern art must be, prescriptions which represent for each artist the duty to acknowledge them while accepting them negatively. But at the same time, a work must be a tool to elucidate its context, a metaphor of the specific conditions which were the basis of its creation. Joseph Beuys is the greatest artist of the latter part of the 20th century for these reasons: he invented an original status for sculpture, breaking away from the former prescriptions dictating what the necessary and sufficient conditions be in order that the sculptor's act be identified as such. Yet more than that, Beuys' work recounted the specific situation in post-1945 Germany. In the same manner, Pollock, Warhol and Ryman have become myths in Europe because we see in them the open crisis in the concept of representation, and its original instrumentation, that is the highest form of expression of American civilization. If in the field of photography, Weston, Evans, Friedlander, and now Baltz are appreciated with so much fidelity in France, it is for the reason that they offer radical points of view indicating, at the level of enlightening metaphor, the general State of the Union.

Panoptic

The ideological overdetermination of an enthusiastic conquest of territory and its riches, simultaneous with the more or less distinct wish for modernity in general under the seal of progress, marks American art as a whole as an enterprise of overexposure. No doubt that its procedures, from exhaustive frontality to serialization, are diverse, but all serve the same obsession of direct visibility: the immediate capture of the object of representation. The history of the visual arts in post-1945 America, be it architecture, sculpture, painting, or photography, has been in the same spirit of the whole in a common project of panoptics. It is an authoritarian position, it is true, which consists of thinking and indicting that everything can, and hence should, be seen. It is an authoritarian position first for the artist concerning himself, which consists of reducing or inhibiting or sublimating all internal conflict, all interior opacity to the periphery of his art; it is an equally authoritarian position in respect to the artist concerning the object of his work, which consists of reducing all negotiation and ambivalence in favor of a direct, linear rapport with its object. In this sense, Lewis Baltz is the worthiest heir to American civilization and rightfully belongs to the history of forceful seeing, of exhaustive faciality, which in the history of American photography is the line from Carleton Watkins to Lewis Baltz, and passes through Steiglitz, Abbott, Weston, Evans, Friedlander, and many other masters of this art. If we consider the already abundant body of work by Baltz which is presented in series (and the concept of the series is extremely pertinent here from *The New Industrial Parks Near Irvine, California*, 1975, through *Candlestick Point*, 1988), what strikes the viewer immediately is precisely this ample and frontal vision in each image,

this predatory observation of each detail, this absolute clarity of perspective which always dominates the representation of the photographic scheme. Moreover, there is a close, though hidden, rapport between Baltz's work and Hans Namuth's images showing the drippings on Jackson Pollock's studio floor: a linear vision which encompasses the entire image as surface and subject.

Because Baltz's subject is space before it is landscape, even in the manner in which the images are ordered within the series and the thematic continuity between one series and the next, there is the approach and instrumentalization of a promised completeness, even though its elements are fragmentary. Everything can and everything must be seen: this is panoptic logic, the logic of modernity: these are the confines, the limits, and the edges that direct us to the observation of the global image. And because Baltz's subject is architecture before it is space, Baltz situates himself in the continuous, worked instant, returning in its passing, and in its return privileging a mental rear-view. His subject is behind him, the better for him to measure its effects before him. This other subject, which is behind him, is the triumphal gesture of American civilization in its entirety: masses, glorious and vertical, as its architecture and land development symbolize it. And it is at exactly this place that we station ourselves before Baltz's work, belonging not to his work but to what determines it. And what we observe from this vantage point is the limit of the triumphal gesture for territorial control (in which we

Shingle, West Vic, 1985 (Collection of Timothy Eaton, Mary Anna Shoen)

participate in varying degrees); this limit we had not wanted, that we had not conceived, and, most of the time, we had not expected. Baltz proposes that this limit be reintegrated in our conception of civilization, as its internal frontier.

Collapse

For the European enamored with his age-old tradition of chiaroscuro, the greatest merit and most eminent success of post-1945 American art resides in the perceived interval between the conquering verticality of a steadfast faith in progress and expansion, and the representation of its collapse. No doubt that everything must always be seen, and accurately. To the enthusiastic elevation of Newman's line which sovereignly distributes the planes of color, there corresponds, like a reverse echo, Pollock's splattered paint. To the ostentatious hymn, to the infinite development of the right angle by Sol Lewitt and certain architects, there is a response in the heterogeneous assemblages of Rauschenberg and the structures of certain other, West Coast, alternative architects. To the lyrical development of David Smith's sculpture corresponds Carl Andre's layouts. To Stella's evolutive post-cubist dynamics is opposed Ryman's neutrality. To Ralph Gibson's formal, flashy seduction is opposed Lewis Baltz's austerity. The examples could go on and on. Everything must be seen, and everything will be, but to those who construct objects which are elaborated to be seen and are exclusively conceived for that purpose are opposed those who determine the consequences concerning this axiom.

In this respect, it is altogether apt that Lewis Baltz proposes to think his work within the register of entropy. On the condition that one realizes that it is a double entropy, an interface where are joined (and this is the major preoccupation of Baltz's work), at their lowest point, two slopes of two probabilities activating this sort of weak, vulgar, common implosion which the photographs represent. The aspect of nature joins the aspect of urbanism on an undefined, atypical and deprived frontier, a frontier where aspects collapse together as they are disseminated one into the other. As is always the case in American art, everything is marvelously transparent here, but what is unusual is that the object of the transparency in Baltz's art is the ultimate opacity of the sign of sterility and extreme finality. Baltz's work is not so removed as it might seem from Warhol's, when the latter multiplies the images of the extreme forefront of production and consumption in its metaphorical forms, that is, death and its representations.

Baltz and Warhol have this in common: the principal subject of their art is the civilization where they work, and when that civilization encounters its points of invalidation, they confer to their work the dimension of a moral gesture while never having the conceit to set forth a moral. Both Warhol and Baltz, perfectly circumspect, absolutely pragmatic, confide to their images the exclusive task of presenting that which is already there, the final term of a process which encircles their point of view and frames the society where they are located.

One may again remark that this ample, varied, and continuous figure of collapse which Lewis Baltz's work sustains is not a burial notice. I mean that there is not a subliminal moral in his work, leaving it up to each viewer the task of supplying it is he so desires. Nor is there a previous moral, either, as we see expressed in some European works, excellent ones to be sure, which could be seen to have some ties with Baltz's: between the beautiful expression of a nostalgia toward old forms of industrial architecture magnificently measured by Bernd and Hilla Becher, and the naturalistic Romanticism of Hamish Fulton's equally fruitful work, in which each image presented conveys a significance which surpasses it. Hence the Bechers' work establishes itself on the basis of a historical moral, of a retrospective vision which confers a function of truth to the classifications which they have erected, working, as they themselves declare, for a redemption of certain forms from the past which they rightly judge unjustly

scorned. In another manner, but equally valuable from the point of view which concerns us, the ever engaging work of Fulton resides in the a priorism of an active and conscious pantheism: nature is the world in parenthesis, simultaneously as process and as representation of a latent truth which the sculptor's method in landscape has as its mission to reveal. Here (in Fulton's work) there is also the redemption of nature as an imminent force which promotes first the categories of space and time: space as a random succession of obstacles; time as the interval of the process between obstacles. For Europeans like us things exist in reality only to the extent that we can hold a prior idea or feeling for them, a pre-existent theory. For Americans it seems that observation comes first, observation which then infers the manner of representation or function.

If we grant a great importance to Lewis Baltz's work here in Europe it is no doubt because we know how to cultivate tact and contact so well, he takes care of impact; if we know how to manage so well the theology of art, the panoptic of collapse presented by Baltz constitutes directions for what Jean-Luc Godard called "an industrialization of the real."

Sculpture

Far be it from me to deny Lewis Baltz his status as a photographer, but his manner of seeing, exclusively turned toward the collapse of identities, leads me to think in the very persistence of this manner he creates a site of virtualities and dissipations which also reflects the history of contemporary

sculpture. When, at the same moment, the reason for land development and the expansion of nature both collapse on the edge of the same site, isn't this dissemination, conjugated in an impalpable interface, also the provisional results of most contemporary sculpture, from the moment that interface becomes material for representation? From Duchamp's ready-mades to the conception of Beuy's social sculpture to Fulton's footsteps, the concept of sculpture has considerably broadened. This is not, however, the place to recount its history. Sculpture today in its most innovative dimension exposes itself in inductive authority, in landmarks of virtualities: the virtuality of space, matter, volume, and transformation. Moreover, to accomplish this it is most often produced by a transfer of the sign and by conversion, withdrawal, and recontextualization. But to appear in this light, sculpture requires a site to situate it, a supposedly institutional transparency which legitimizes its opacity or its vacuity. Grease by Beuys, pavings by Andre, shredded rubber or steel plates by Serra, land movements by Smithson, trash cans by Arman, bundles of sticks by Merz: these are so many indications which to have a value as such require the indicating support of the great extendible show window of the museum, which extends itself in our interiors and in our minds. Certainly Baltz's work is above all the unforgettable trace of a disjunctive synthesis between nature and culture, together forbidden in a structure where all qualities are dissipated. And I would conjecture that Lewis Baltz, the sculptor, proceeds in this general framework, which is the photographer's, pointing with intelligence and humor to the collapse of modern sculpture, to its dissemination, and to the commutation of all of its distinctive traits in a sort of general random crisis which marks the end of the power of reification and, equally, the end of the theology of art.

An important work of modern art always appears as a synthesis, a closure, a definitive obstacle, or impassible threshold. Let's look carefully at all of Lewis Baltz's series while keeping in mind the sculpture and environmental department of the modern art museum. Everything is there, but has imploded, is dilapidated, scattered about and, once again, collapsed. For Baltz, sculpture is scattered details, discrete traits of distribution, temporary limits within a deficient space. The proposition is definite; it is sovereign because it provokes laughter. One has in mind the formidable preparations of all those masterpieces by Serra, Arman, Keinholz, Kaprow, Morris, Beuys, Heizer, Merz, etc.? They are all there, recognizable, but moved from their places of privilege into the milieu, and from this center to the frontiers. How does modernity disappear? By pulverization and contamination. Everything is modern; hence nothing, no longer is. Modernity no longer needs to be a social commandment or a personal prescription, since it establishes itself as such, according to its own criteria, even in the border zones where its force no longer holds. Even more serious, modernity is no longer the experimental act of a subject; it always establishes itself distinctively in the random rebounds of the anonymous manipulations on its margin.

No doubt one must be the greatest and the last modern American photographer to elaborate the experience of the historical collapse on the internal edge of our societies where all the real questions are posed at last.

Bernard Lamarche-Vadel
Paris 1990
translated by William Wheeler

CONTINUOUS FIRE POLAR CIRCLE

Near Deadline, Nevada

"When the artist goes to the desert he enriches his absence
and burns off the water on his brain."

Robert Smithson

Baltz's portfolio, called *Near Reno*, is clearly akin to such other of his well-known works as *Park City*, *San Quentin Point*, and *Nevada*, the latter from 1977. In each, the artist scans a landscape in which the conflict between nature and culture is clearly in evidence, and yet not so clearly drawn in terms of right and wrong. One senses a mutually devolving relation of hillsides to houses, of erosion to construction, of trash to landfill. The ethics of urban blight and the ethicless natural conditions of entropy and decay are somehow flip sides of a coin, conspirators on a grand scale. It was not surprising, then, that Baltz would choose to scan the periphery of Reno in search of the kinds of cooly ironic sites that frame the incidental collisions between human and other nature, and which mark the landscape like drying wounds—the kinds of post-industrial "non-sites" Robert Smithson saw as evidence of a primordial tug on civilization's infrastructure. In this sense, *Near Reno* is similar to Baltz's previous bodies of work.

The new works scan a landscape that is more like a battlefield than an entropic plain, and the staging of each image is therefore more urgent in the story it, and each of its prior and subsequent images, seems to tell. Of course, terms such as "urgent" are unusual in relation to Baltz's photographs which are more usually cool and understated, even to the point of some loss of irony, a flatness which is apropos of his devolving subjects. But within Baltz's particular range of low intensity drama, these pictures do suggest a kind of past-tense violence in which the sites are restaged as "scenes of the crime," places we come upon and are forced to read in terms of clues and residual effects. Scattered far and wide from their identifying contexts, the stuff which rests there—the old appliances, piles of dirt, and dead animals—attests to a deep severance, like fragments for which wholes cannot be re-imagined. This field of residual effects is a kind of second-order landscape, analogous to the periphery of thought. And while Baltz has often staged the overlooked, it is, I think, fair to say that with *Near Reno* he has sighted evidence of some prior violence which is more disturbing in its implications.

One feels differently, for example, about a washing machine that rusts than about one which is blasted apart. Such sites not only represent the material overspill of an ever-obsolete society, but they also show signs of the kinds of anti-social impulses—like simulating movie violence by shooting bottles filled with red paint—that are otherwise inappropriate to city life. They are the places of an aggressive—yet somehow sadly impotent—psychological overflow which targets already dead, already useless things, and are fittingly on the fringes of cities whose cores are riddled with violence that is real. Dumpsites as Saturday morning comic book combat zones for adult men with guns. A new "pop!" art? Perhaps such places represent a residual romanticism in search of "intense" and "authentic" experience—something like a new (literal) landscape painting, the ground awash in latex around bits of broken glass.

Earlier, I said that Baltz's pictures "seemed" to tell a story. They induce a narrative rhythm and imply thematic bridges from one to another, and back. But they do not tell a story *per se*. Instead, the rather abbreviated left-to-right sequence of these fourteen photographs sets up a narrative expectation which is undermined by the basically equivocal relations among the images. It's as if each subject, whether a terraced hillside, a blasted soda can, or a dead sheep, were equally unimportant. The result is a dramatic flatness. No peaks, no valleys. Only mounds.

Baltz is telling a story of sorts with and about pictures of marginal things—things now defunct, wasted, and destroyed, but occasionally recognizable enough to carry in themselves a kind of memory of what they used to be and do. A soda can riddled with bullets, the white tin back of some appliance (a washing machine?), a shattered TV set, a freshly dead sheep crawling with raisin-size flies, a dying bush—things which have been changed in a way that diminishes them, or which, in some cases, strips away even their most marginal identities so that they seem ripped from the contexts by which we might have known them and deposited into the condition known only as waste. Most of these pictures are of profoundly displaced things, and they are displaced on multiple levels: as to function, as to place, as to appearance, as to time. And this forces the ironic displacement of photographic focus—of artistic attention—upon unresponsive subjects. Baltz spends a lot of energy framing and composing things which, both visually and dramatically, go flat in the pictures, a flatness which deflates the representational authority of the photographic frame, as if it were somehow misapplied. And therein lies a powerful double displacement of both the photographic subject and the focus of its object, a displacement which sweeps these pictures to what might be called the backside of traditional landscape photography. *Near* photography, as the roadsides, dumpsites, and fenceposts are near Reno.

Baltz uses his focus as a kind of perceptual blade to cut through his subjects—and, consequently, the photographic field—at particularly undramatic points: a withering tree near a roadside, a swath of grass and gravel on the ground, or a cluster of tumbleweeds in the desert. As it slips from infinity in the first (photographs a diptych of Reno from afar) to the glaring surface of subsequent ones, this displaced focus becomes a way of insisting upon *something* in a picture of virtual non things, a crystalline slice of photographic vision, the camera's eye, lost among piles of unimportant stuff out near the edges of town. The more one thinks about Baltz's displacement of focus, the more his whole portfolio begins to seem like a metaphor for the displacement of photography itself, away from the center and toward the periphery, where things lose themselves: out-of-focus spheres where both the subjects and their objects of representation seem fuzzy.

Baltz practices a kind of anti-narrative in which certain of his subjects' ripe implications teeter from picture to picture *in both directions*, so that the reading of one image affects not only its successor, but also its predecessor. Beginning with a diptych i.e., with a 19th century desert panorama as a kind of springboard—the artist quickly scales down to dumpsite proportions through an image of a terraced hillside, then to a dump. In this inelegant decline, the idea of landscape falls through successive layers of artificiality, disuse, and scale, ending up a residual heap on the ground. Thus, the idea of a *substitute landscape* is introduced, and our re-reading of the initial diptych adjusts accordingly. No longer a panorama, the visage is one from outside looking in, its hillsides all in the foreground, its subject—Reno—over the edge, unseen, its focus lost in the glare of a vast Nevada light.

And then there's a television set on the ground, its screen caved in by a rock, reclaimed, so to speak, by the landscape, naturalized. And yet, is the rock not now a picture? A scaled-down panorama on (literally in) TV? And is the TV not a metaphor for the photographic frame? The photographic field? With the television in the land, and the land in the television, is not, then, this picture of the mutual and endless interpolation of landscape and its frame, like an infinite string of images in a barbershop mirror? One thinks back several frames, and realizes that the mountains have been reduced to a rock inside a box, a commentary on our consciousness of the natural world if ever there was one.

Several frames ahead, we come upon a dead sheep, tilted up, like an offering, on a sandy ground. It is covered with healthy flies. Thinking back, the previous image—that of a barren swath of gravel and glass—now seems like a clean plate, like a place *before* the sheep, ready to receive it. Looking ahead, we see the tin-white back of a washing machine, shot full of holes, and the holes, which are opening at us, suddenly look like flies. Hinged at the top of the picture, the white metal sheet leans toward us, much like the sheep, which may also have been shot. In this sequence, it's as if the picture plane was assaulting us.

There are other sequential patterns, and they build and diminish both forward and back. None is really dominant, and the slippage among them denotes a certain entropy, a narrative leveling-out. Baltz does not idealize his subjects in order to secure our empathy, but he sets his focus to wandering in a manner analogous to the devolving condition of our new late 20th century landscapes: those which are residual, artificial, peripheral, violent, unseen. Out near deadline. A kind of second nature.

If archaeologists scout the dumpsites of past civilizations, then contemporary artists are sometimes archaeological in their investigations, providing historians with contemporaneous comments on the sites which will someday be sifted, full of junk which will someday be valuable. In fact, such art may also take its place in the sites which ring our cities—or, more likely, they will settle into the sites we've set aside for the tribal ornaments we somehow want to keep, but for which we have no other place: museums, the sites of displaced history.

Perhaps, sometime in the future, the black portfolio case for Baltz's photographs will be as interesting as the photographs themselves. About the size of an important book, it has, nearer the top than the middle, the words "NEAR RENO" embossed on its face in a candy-apple red. One thinks of a whorehouse at night. Or the words become a street map of Reno, its casinos beaming in a cheap gaseous light. I've seen this sight before—Reno from a distance, or from the air, a glow beyond the horizon. Something about which to reflect. Someplace we are not, but which follows us. And as Lewis Baltz has shown us, a place makes another kind of sense from the edge.

Jeff Kelley
Arlington, Texas, 1987

NEAR RENO

Near Reno, #1

Near Reno, #2

Wasteland: A Précis

This is terrain. Vast and indistinct, yet bounded by its three horizons: a plateau of shallow sandstone, a dry plain, a bright bay; predictably for flat terrain, the skies are vast. Its components are stagnant and heavy: stony soils, pools and swamps, salt marshes, scabby ground. White light holding sway, air burns, troubled with vibration lines and possible mirage. Except that north winds funnel through the valley and sweep across the delta, filling it with passing purity. Or on the other hand, that sea winds bring in ochre sands from far-off deserts.

That time, on the borders of this steppe with its ponds and sea, a Roman soldier kneaded in glory and flanked by a Pythian of doubtful oracle built the first settlements. Fresh or seawater anglers worked the wind, patient shots were fired at migrating birds, and ploughpersons of rare arable soils engendered gradual boroughs long deprived of progress, "the great heresy of decrepitude" in Baudelaire's virtuous phrase. One fine day, a great fever of enterprise seized hold of personkind and the bay shore; it hollowed out harbors and ports, built dikes, embankments, and reservoirs, transformed energy and matter. Laid lines, fixed limits, zones and sectors.

Between the dotted lines, in shading and in hieroglyphics—codes—an inaenuous future anticipated incredible matter, endless combinations, infinite variations, amalgam and precipitate, structure and process, products whose manna were to fall back in flakes on the delta. Heavy ships hugging the waters would work toward the shore the finite chain of carbons, its chlorides, styrenes, propylenes, and liquid-crystal polymers—an endless spiral, joyous and fecund.

Natural space would juxtapose to these places devolved to the purely synthetic. Sowing, planting, grafting, thinning and spraying for resistance to frosts and drought, to spindrift, salt, lime, fluorides, hydrochloric acid, hydrogen sulphur, nitrogen oxide—growth, rapid enough, gradual enough or gradual; in bearing fastigiate or pyramid-like; a regular treeline perhaps, persistent foliage. And in these barren wastes—*ah bear in mind this garden never was enchanted*—the silver cedar, bald cypress and umbrellla pine, the Judas and the locust tree, the pubescent oak, white ash, Bohemian olive, tamarisk and varnish sumac would spring up. . . .

Birds of the swamp and lagoon (mallard or pochard, coot, moorhen, stilt, purple heron, marsh, reed or fan-tailed warbler, egret, crested grebe, redshank, avocet and herring-gull, tern, flamingo and Kentish plover) would be joined by the hummingbird, toucan and bird of paradise; there would be palm groves, silver birches, walnut trees, kangaroos, ant bears, giraffes, white tigers from Siberia. Man's industry is capable of anything—even the arch.

Man is versatile, changeable, capricious. No sooner had they embarked on the great adventure than they began to lose interest. Turning to other tasks, they moved on to new fates, abandoned the water-tanks, complex silver-coated ducts, a blazing torch which might have made Apollo turn pale, ground torn between the past and the future.

Upon a rocky mound a church of timeworn stone and a tiny, idyllic graveyard; outside the village cafes, quiet, obese old men, knees agape under cast-iron tables, rehearse local gossip. Pungent, milky liquids hover on trays that highlight hairy chests and pinned gold crosses. Children run down to sea scattered with tottering colorful sails. The odor of sulphur dioxide hangs everywhere. Sector 80 stretches out some distance from a beach of Eden (nudists only). What is to be her special fate? Is she waiting for jetties thrust out into the bay? Swagger of chimneys, bright facades? Blue-thread overalls, sirens awail?

Fos Secteur 80 (installation at Flemish Cultural Center, Alden Biessen Castle, Belgium) photo: Daniele Tanto (p 113); *Near Reno, #6* (pp 110/111)

"Literature (and art) is what suddenly reminds us of the true state of the world," said Jean Paulhan, a vaguely northern neighbor of this place. Sector 80, conquered and abandoned, a strip of land marked with the trace of massive machines, the scoriæ of furtive camps, touching cast-offs of human enterprise, fragments of asphalt, rusty cans, the necks of polythene bottles, uprooted stumps, breeze-blocks arrayed like a ritual *kiwa*, zinc pipes and totems, rags soaked and mummified—stiff as antique shrouds. Strange weeds, dense shrubs and prickly plants finding their way through the upturned, scooped out, vitrified soil. No wild grasses in these harsh locations. Well-behaved, indifferent plants, corseted within impenetrable stalks. Tenacious, stubborn, defiant life-forms, as after a cataclysm. But no pessimism in the spectacle of Sector 80. The state of the place. The true condition of the world.

Olivier Boissière
Paris, 1987
translated by Kenneth Hylton

Fos Secteur 80, (1 element); *Fos Secteur 80*, (2 elements) (p 115)

Space begins because we look away from where we are...

"asking after of before"   Michael Palmer, *Sun* from a poem "Baudelaire Series"

Flats

Look across, missing what the gaze travels over to get from unnoticed here to a more distant present, the one way over there, and there, and on, there. Head like a transit, look out at, look around and over to and across, finding boundaries only in the far haze: north, the southern outskirts of the city marked by a huge electrical tower: east, the shipyard crane and inhabited shoreline across a bay; on south to the unseen international airport; and then westerly, back around again, to the gigantic sports stadium. These are the boundaries of this vast, flat place without sides, as if a volcanic cone had eroded to expose this floor that exposes everything on it. These photographs study the peculiar flatness of Candlestick Point. They think about our exposure here. The presiding mood is flat; infrequent interruptions of this horizon are depressions (gulleys, ditches, backwaters) and elevations that are dump sites pushed up and rounded off by the wakes and bow-waves of crawler-tracked machines and bulldozers. Domestic and industrial materials alike are discarded here. They build this wasteland that was constructed so we might forget.

The jetsam identities of pilings and ties, and dumps of rubble and heaps of masonry debris, the piles of scrap metal and wood shavings resemble the materials and subject matter of much contemporary sculpture (Smithson, Heizer, Chamberlain, Di Suvero). They test these enterprises, a wasted reality raising the questions art forgoes. Candlestick Point is a place as apart as cemeteries, national parks, civic plazas—an underbelly of the sublime, where the wasted challenges the composed. Who's real?

An unobstructed view, one that nobody seems to command. How to command a clear view when it appears that there is nothing to be seen. That is what is depicted, *the nothing seen*, what it looks like once it is noticed and brought into view. A deep interior of flatness, one adjacent to the one Chauncey Hare reveals. This one is under the floorboards and foundations of where we build, what we reclaim and what we would forget. Space begins because we look away from where we are. We could not do that were space not already begun, there before us, enabling us, a flatness in our lives that discovers horizons. We look away. These photographs make us look again. We do and never look quite the same way again, a little less spaced out than before, beginning our inevitable return.

Candlestick Point (installation Castelli Graphics, New York, 1989); photo: Nicholas Walster, courtesy Castelli Graphics (pp 116/117)

Bracket, a narrative foldout

[*Imagine the following pages of a book, beginning with photograph 21; turn the page; now 22 and 25 are facing pages; 25 covers 23 and when you open out the fold 23 pans right to 24 while 22, 23, 24 together now form a triptych which 25 covers, enclosing or bracketing 23, 24 by again facing 22.*]

to hillocks and shoulders, crests and troughs and berms of cross-ties and pilings, scrap lumber and demolished billboards; piles of tires linked by a circular object to a pile of metal scrap; a mattress on the ground with a headboard of unmortared bricks, scattered here and there one-brick courses stacked three and four bricks high. who sleeps there? who built the little unprotective foundation? what dream of masonry informs the stacks of bricks?

pilings and ties tossed atop heaps of shavings that extend towards (25): a coil of electric wire hung over the end of a beam, an empty metal drawer, on a crooked branch a flag collapsed of peace or surrender, and in the center, bordered by wrecked pilasters, a picket fence topped with a madcap of dried palm branches, as if out of domestic catastrophe waste might yet dream itself a home?

Bracket, the poem of the foldout

What narrative? As I wrote, on one poem, a part of it, kept repeating itself in me. Here are the revealing fragments, perfect appositions

> *By the road to the contagious hospital*
> *under the surge of the blue*
> *mottled clouds driven from the*
> *northeast—a cold wind. Beyond, the*
> *waste of broad muddy fields*
> *brown with dried weeds, standing and fallen*
>
> *patches of standing water*
> *the scattering of tall trees*
>
> *All along the road the reddish*
> *purplish, forked, upstanding, twiggy*
> *stuff of bushes and small trees*
> *with dead, brown leaves under them*
> *leafless vines—*

William Carlos Williams
from *Spring and All*

The seventh stanza is too perfect to be left out. Included in this fragmentation it reads:

> *One by one objects are defined—*
> *It quickens: clarity. . .*

As I turned the pages, opening and closing the petals of the foldouts, returning again and again to the photographs, to *Candlestick Point*, I kept on knowing the justice of Williams' words. How could they not be included?

Clarity quickens unapologetic apposition.

51

The camera creates a tree where none is. An angle does it, the photographer's position toward what is present.

Starting from the top, the photograph (51) shows leaves and the branches of a eucalyptus. The central bough crowns a smooth, exfoliated trunk that turns out to be an abandoned electrical pole. A dangling wire trails sketchily down its right side, unattached to an iron electrical ground. Rubble strews the foreground. A chain-link skirt, protecting it from what?, encircles the base of the pole.

Trees break the level of this prostrate place where elevations and depressions alike still leave you in the dumps. There are very few trees in this place, stadia breaking the horizontal or odd dustball shapes at the end of an otherwise horizonless plain. A small stand of trees cluster around a sprawling concrete pad; they are deteriorating, sickly, dying, dead.

The angle crowns with leaves *not even* a dead tree. The camera memorializes a vast absence of trees in their own former materials. This tree is not a tree, not even the memory of a tree, or its trace. This photograph creates a tree where none is, out of the materials of a tree, the photographic equivalent of a field-stripped, exploded-view drawing of? a weapon? a tree? The photograph constructs itself and its content as an artificial ruin (a folly) and thinks about consequences, about futures: by showing us another cap of madness on a visionary face—the expression of affliction memorialized by the always open face of the world.

Candlestick Point, 1988 (element #51) (detail) (p 121)

It colors, obscuring

The contrasts are tonal, not stark. Color brings nothing closer. When we think about color we think it has to bring the world closer. Yet it neutralizes distance. This color in particular, since it is commercial, continues the presence of the mechanical in photography. The machine rolls on manufacturing the colors we think of as realer. Than? than other colors? As in the color, so in the sentence: something is missing. We are what is missing; we are who are out of it, not just *left* out, but out altogether. How does color declare our absence?. . . yet it neutralizes distance, spreads things out and up and across. Color flattens, it is the shadow cast by a lost dramatic art. *Color*, Newton said, *comes after* (the experiment in the dark room was not about the spectrum but about the different refrangibility of the rays that comprise the bundle of light—Hume, introducing his fantasies of this method into philosophy, discovered that passively we are bundles of perceptions; then self *comes after*....After *whom?*) Goethe, looking through a prism in a lighted room, saw chromatic abberations, and thinking of what Newton had done to make light color—bent it, in the dark, through a crystal prism— said, *Color is the suffering of light.* Other alchemists trace colors' origins to bitterness, in particular to salt. Color is presentiment. Were colors to fade we would see the (bad) photograph underneath; were the photograph to fade we would be left with film like a cataract or like the eye of a dead television set. Color is fugitive. It flees what it depicts and takes the subject with it. Color is tantalizing. The distance it places between us is our own idea of our perception. (*We see the world in color.* A peculiar assertion.) Color is sensuous only because it extirpates the senses and discards the flesh, both the necessary conditions of its appearance. It destroys the conditions that create it. *That* is the condition interposed. In these photographs our absence is essential. Color here heralds the conditions that include the human only as commercial, qualified for a mortgage and willing to build and purchase, the scene transformed before the players and counters enter—enter a scene that is constructed to exclude them. It colors. The contrasts are starker than tone. Color is plotless.

Nothing has colored it. The site colors. We long to see the world in black and white. But it colors. Color comes between me, myself, I and others, casting out all of us. It seems we can do nothing to prevent our perceptions interfering with our souls, tossing aside our bodies, making us but one more thing among all the colored things, nothing outstanding. Color shows us how we have lost our way and cannot find our way back through it. The machine rolls on. The world wears commercial colors and is beyond recall. We do not know which side of it (color) we are on because it all looks the same. Everything is in color yet we still feel a difference, an important one lost, while we struggle and while our perception escapes us and returns against us, behind our backs and before our faces—the world keeps on coloring. Color puts us in orbit. It colors, goes on coloring, and ends, colored. Color flays the skin of the world. We hang it up to dry. So it comes between us and ourselves.

for Felice Gonzales
Gus Blaisdell
Albuquerque, 1988

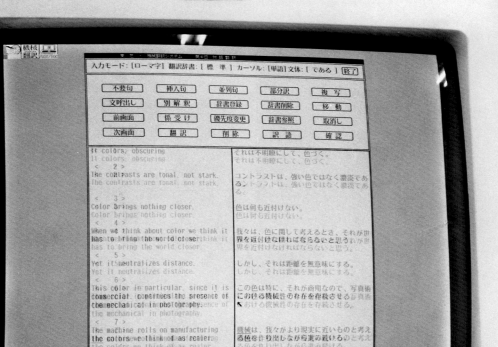

Pleasure Cruiser Blows Up; Financier and Wife Killed

No'
3
[Ri]ey

16. (AP)
[M]arshall
[Rus]sian re-
[disc]ussions
[forei]gn Min-
[fixed] for a
[o]n Ger-
[-e]conom-
[e]rs said
[su]ccess or
[i]c-power

[d]ay, new-
[c]ommand-
[i]n Eu-
[ro]w from
[wh]en Mar-
[sh]al talks.
[turn]ed down
[Molo]tal-
[tu]ral talks.
[e]xchange
[of] British
[info]rmation
[situ]ation.

[ad]ded
[th]at Mar-
[ch]ange the
[a]nd that
[ro]be con-
[e]mitments
[to] confer-
[en]clude any
[o]f internal

[s]aid For-
[e] expect-
[in] the
[fa]ll.

[d]ivid-
[susp]ect the
[o]ne most
[sen]ce. The
[uni]ty and
[conside]red the
[Germ]an prob-

[wi]nter-
[n]ational
[ph]ase
[nego]tiation. If
[n] these,

Daughter See[s] Tragedy in Newport Bay

Walter E. Overell, 62, [re-] tired furniture executive a[nd] owner of the Washington [Fi-] nance Co., and his socia[lly] prominent wife Beulah, were killed instantly shor[tly] before midnight Saturday [in] an explosion which shatte[red] their 47-foot cabin cru[iser] Mary E in Newport Harb[or.]

Missing death by minu[tes,] their 17-year-old daughter, B[eu-] lah Louise, and a friend, Geo[rge] Gallum of 2301 Carmona A[ve.,] had rowed ashore on an err[and] just prior to the blast and st[ood] horror-stricken on the d[ock] while the Mary E shuddered [and] settled by the bow, witne[sses] said.

The boat was moored 150 [feet] off the foot of B St., about [half] way between a residential [sec-] tion of the Balboa peninsula [and] Balboa Island.

First on Scene

First to reach the stric[ken] craft was a retired Los Ang[eles] fireman, F. E. Moore of [ ] Silverlake Blvd., who was [a-] board his boat Bello Cam[ ] moored 75 yards away.

"It just about blew me [out] of my bunk," Moore said [of the] blast.

Moore jumped into his [boat] and rowed to the Mary E. [He] found the forward cabin [was] full of water and could see [no] sign of life. He was joined [in] his rescue efforts by Miss O[ver-] ell and her companion and [the] crew of a Coast Guard pa[trol] boat under the command [of] Motor Machinist's Mate Ro[bert] V. Meyers, but the bodies w[ere] not located until the craft [had] been towed to shallow water [at] the foot of B St.

Laid to Gasoline

Newport Beach Fire C[hief] Frank Crocker said the ex[plo-] sion apparently was caused [by] gasoline and that the couple [died] instantly in the cruiser's ca[bin.]

SHATTERED—Newport Beach firemen and Coast Guardsmen examine 47-foot cruiser Mary E after explosion which killed Walter E. Overell, retired furniture executive and financier, and his wife Beulah Saturday night in Newport Harbor.

Times photo

Quake Shakes
[Illinois Section]

MERCURY DIPS 13 DEGREES TO NICE COOL 7[ ]

Surging Wave
[E]ngulfs Seven

Berlin, March, 1989

Dear Lewis,

It is very difficult to write about the work of a friend, especially when one is as close a friend as you.

Sometimes there is the danger of being too benevolent or, on the other hand, too critical, and I speak of that from experience as far as you are concerned.

We got to know each other in 1980 in Berlin. We invited you. You, elegant and with oriental politeness, I a little shoddy and blunt. I found that a good mixture.

During hors d'oeuvres, I said that an image by you reminded me of Robert Adams, or I said did Adams do that? That's when you got into your element and insisted that it was something altogether different. Naturally you were right, had it not been for the damned beautiful quality of photography: I mean that image-wise. In short, we plunged into drinking, arguing and we were all drunk with photography and wine.

Immediately we had the same madness and passion for photography in common and the readiness to exchange ideas. Both of us had the ambition to discover photography anew. Our secret point of view was: Photography is dead; long live Photography!

You were interested in European photography, I in American. We loved Robert Adams' *The New West*; you alone loved the Bechers. I found it good, but too Prussian. Understandable, I think, for one who was born here. But attitude and consequence have a high value as far as the work of the Bechers goes, and because of that I can understand your admiration of their work.

Back then we were in the position of children of separation, I think, where one parent went to America and the other stayed in Europe. We had the choice of where to go, but as Romantics we thought we could have both.

As with every good artist, you are deeply moral. I'll get right to the point:

Your honesty has always impressed me. Sometimes you have employed that as a weapon of self-defense, but never as one of offense. Your seriousness has been concerned with love, death, and despair, and that means that failure has something to do with it. That, I find, is your greatness. You are passionately excited about images. Earlier in America you stood up for our images. I thank you for that.

Today, Lewis, you have become more quiet and moderate. But the interior, as far as your work is concerned, is severe, with doubts and insecurities.

It always strikes me that the more the images say, the less their creators have to say. You can't have it both ways, but that's not necessary. Now as ever, you are working hard. As far as I can remember, you have always photographed the same thing, utilizing the object for the purpose of always newly realizing your conception of photography. First your images showed substance; later you reduced everything to the vacuousness of the cold machine eye. That again was substance—the substance provided by the camera: cold, merciless, the surface of things reflected. You began to meld with the camera. The unkind, cold gaze—exactly that that the camera can do—became the focal point of your work.

In your new work you have left that in the past. Your outlook becomes more important. From my vantage point you are making your best images today. Not that your earlier work was bad, but there are fruits which are best eaten when ripe. *Prost*, Lewis !

When I consider your books, I am reminded that with each book you correct the previous ones. This reveals a candor and perhaps dissatisfaction with accomplishments. Your books relay an outlook that has structure but no dogmatic concept. That's what life is. Your work is theory that you formulate from possibility and not from truth. That does not make it any less true. I send my hearty greetings to you from Berlin.

Your Michael

Michael Schmidt
translated by Robert C. Fuller

Lewis Baltz

Born Newport Beach, California, 12 September 1945; Bachelor of Fine Arts, San Francisco Art Institute, 1969; Master of Fine Arts, Claremont Graduate School, California, 1971; Individual Fellowship, National Endowment for the Arts, 1973 and 1977; John Simon Guggenheim Memorial Fellowship, 1977; United States-United Kingdom Bicentennial Exchange Fellowship, 1980. Lives and works in California and Europe.

Chronology of Works and Projects

The Highway Series, 1967-1969; *The Tract Houses*, 1969-71; *The Public Places*, 1973; *The New Industrial Parks Near Irvine, California*, 1974-75; *Maryland*, 1976; *Nevada*, 1977; *Park City*, 1978-80; *San Quentin Point*, 1981-83; *The Canadian Series*, 1984; *Continuous Fire Polar Circle*, 1985; *Near Reno*, 1986; *Fos Secteur 80*, 1987; *Candlestick Point*, 1984-88; Untitled rejected proposal for Newport Harbor Art Museum, California, 1989 to present; *Technologies*, 1989 to present.

Monographs

The New Industrial Parks Near Irvine, California, Castelli Graphics, New York, 1975; *Maryland*, essay by Jane Livingston, The Corcoran Gallery of Art, Washington, D.C., 1976; *Nevada*, Castelli Graphics, New York, 1978; *Park City*, with Gus Blaisdell, Aperture, Inc., New York, 1978; *San Quentin Point*, essay by Mark Haworth-Booth, Aperture, Inc., New York, in association with Verlag Zwolftes-Haus, Berlin, and Éditions littéraires et artistiques/La Différence, Paris, 1986; *Candlestick Point*, essay by Gus Blaisdell, Gallery Min, Tokyo, 1989.

Selected Individual Exhibitions

1992: Los Angeles County Museum of Art. *1991*: Des Moines Art Center, Iowa; John and Mable Ringling Museum of Art, Sarasota, Florida; Mills College Art Gallery, Oakland, California; Castelli Graphics, New York. *1990*: Institute for Contemporary Art, P.S. 1 Museum, Long Island City, New York. *1989*: Castelli Graphics, New York; Lorence-Monk, New York; Gallery Min, Tokyo. *1988*: Galerie Michèle Chomette, Paris; Higashikawa-ku City Museum, Japan. *1987*: Galerie Éspace l'Orient, Lorient, France; Tokyo Institute of Polytechnics. *1986*: Newport Harbor Art Museum, California; Eaton/Shoen Gallery, San Francisco; Sierra Nevada Museum of Art, Reno. *1985*: Castelli Graphics, New York; Victoria and Albert Museum, London; Galerie Michèle Chomette, Paris; Werkstatt für Photographie, Berlin; University of New Mexico, Albuquerque. *1984*: University Art Museum, University of California, Berkeley; University of Victoria, British Columbia. *1983*: Castelli Graphics, New York; Rhode Island School of Design, Providence. *1981*: Castelli Graphics, New York; San Francisco Museum of Modern Art; Otis Art Institute of Parsons School of Design, Los Angeles. *1980*: Werkstatt für Photographie, Berlin; Galerie Fiolet, Amsterdam. *1979*: Nova Scotia College of Art and Design, Halifax. *1978*: Castelli Graphics, New York; Yarlow-Salzman Fine Arts, Toronto; University of Nevada, Reno. *1976*: Museum of Fine Arts, Houston, Texas; The Corcoran Gallery of Art, Washington, D.C.; Baltimore Museum of Art, Maryland; La Jolla Museum of Contemporary Art, California; Galerie December, Düsseldorf. *1975*: Leo Castelli Gallery, New York; Philadelphia College of Art, Pennsylvania; University of New Mexico, Albuquerque. *1974*: Corcoran Gallery of Art, Washington, D.C. *1973*: Castelli Graphics, New York. *1972*: International Museum of Photography at George Eastman House, Rochester, New York. *1971*: Castelli Graphics, New York.

Kawasaki 1A and 1B, 1989, courtesy Toshiba Project (pp 126/127), *Kawasaki 2A and 2B*, 1989, courtesy Toshiba Project (pp 128/129), *Rule Without Exception*, 1988 (pp 130/131), *Piazza Sigmund Freud*, 1989 (three elements) (pp 132/133, 134/135, 136/137), collection of the John and Mable Ringling Museum of Art, Sarasota, Florida; From a study for a proposal for the Newport Harbor Art Museum, 1989 (p 138)

Selected Group Exhibitions

1990: *Signs of Life: Process and Materials, 1960-1990*, Institute of Contemporary Art, University of Pennsylvania, Philadelphia, catalogue; *The New American Pastoral: Landscape Photography In the Age of Questioning*, International Museum of Photography at George Eastman House, Rochester, New York, circulating to Whitney Museum of American Art at Equitable Center, New York. *D'un art L'autre*, La Vieille Charité et les Musées de Marseille, France, catalogue; *Structures and Shelters*, Rena Bransten Gallery, San Francisco.

1989: *La Lumière du Temps*, Fonds Régional d'Art Contemporain Bretagne, Chateaugiron, France, catalogue; *Photography Now*, Victoria and Albert Museum, London, catalogue; *On the Art of Fixing a Shadow: One Hundred and Fifty Years of Photography*, National Gallery of Art, Washington,. D.C., The Art Institute of Chicago and Los Angeles County Museum of Art, catalogue; *The Presence of Photographs in the Learning of Urban and Territorial Projects*, School of Architecture, Politecnico of Milan; *Trends 89*, Kawasaki City Museum, Japan, catalogue; *Landscape*, International Seminar, Alden Biessen, Belgium.

1988: *Evocative Presence*, Museum of Fine Arts, Houston, Texas, catalogue; *Dag Alveng/Lewis Baltz*, Museet for Photokunst, Odense, Denmark; *Castelli Graphics 1969-1988*, Castelli Graphics, New York.

1987: *Dialectical Landscapes: Nuovo Passagio Americano*, Palazzo Fortuny, Museo e Centro di Documentazione Fotografica, Venice, catalogue; *Preoccupations*, Victoria and Albert Museum, London; *American Dreams*, Centro Reina Sofia, Madrid, catalogue; *Modern Photography and Beyond*, National Museum of Modern Art, Kyoto, catalogue; *Photography and Art*, Los Angeles County Museum of Art, The Queens Museum, New York, and Des Moines Art Center, Iowa, catalogue; *Recent Acquisitions*, The Museum of Modern Art, New York; *Lewis Baltz: RENO/Anthony Hernandez: LAS VEGAS*, University of Nevada, Las Vegas, and University of Nevada, Reno, catalogue; *Von Landschaftbild zur Spürensicherung*, Museum Ludwig, Köln, catalogue.

1986: *The Real Big Picture*, The Queens Museum, New York; *Californie*, Galerie Michèle Chomette, Paris; *Facets of Modernism*, San Francisco Museum of Modern Art; *New Acquisitions, New Landscapes*, Victoria and Albert Museum, London; *Ansel Adams and American Landscape Photography*, Australian National Gallery, Canberra, catalogue; *Views and Visions*, The Aldrich Museum of Contemporary Art, Ridgefield, Connecticut.

1985: *American Images*, Barbican Art Gallery, London, circulating, catalogue; *Joe Bishop AIDS Benefit*, Richard Kuhlenschmidt Gallery, Los Angeles; *Paris-New York-Tokyo*, Tsukuba Museum, Japan, catalogue; *Symposion über Photographie*, Forumstadtpark, Graz, Austria; *Images of Excellence*, International Museum of Photography at George Eastman House, Rochester, New York, circulating, catalogue; *Robert Adams, Lewis Baltz, Joel Sternfeld: Three Photographers of the Man-Altered Landscape*, Graduate School of Design, Harvard University, Cambridge, Massachusetts; *Second-Site: Major Works*, Eaton/Shoen Gallery, San Francisco.

1984: *The Automobile and Culture*, The Museum of Contemporary Art, Los Angeles and Detroit Art Institute, Michigan, catalogue; *Fifteenth Anniversary Exhibition*, Castelli Graphics, New York; *La Photographie Creative*, Pavillon des Arts de la Ville de Paris; *Photography in California, 1945-1980*, San Francisco Museum of Modern Art, circulating, catalogue; *Construire les Paysages de la Photographie: 21 Auteurs et Plasticiens Contemporain*, Caves St. Croix, Metz, France, circulating, catalogue; *3-Dimensional Photographs/3-Dimensional Paintings*, Carl Solway Gallery, Cincinnati, Ohio.

1983: *3-Dimensional Photographs*, Castelli Graphics, New York; *L'architecture: Sujet, Objet, ou Pretexte*, Musée des Beaux-Arts, Agen, France, circulating, catalogue; *3-Dimensional Photographs*, Hermann Wunsche Gallery, Bonn; *Photography and the Industrial Image*, The Grey Art Gallery and Study Center, New York University .

1982: *International Photography 1920-1980*, Australian National Gallery, Canberra, catalogue; *Urban America*, San

Francisco Museum of Modern Art; *Space Framed*, Graduate School of Design, Harvard University, Cambridge, Massachusetts; *Symposion über Photographie*, Forumstadtpark, Graz, Austria; *Urban Vernacular*, Henry Art Gallery, University of Washington, Seattle.

1981: *New Topographics*, Arnolfini Gallery, Bristol, England, circulating, catalogue; *A Sense of Order*, Institute of Contemporary Art, University of Pennsylvania, Philadelphia, catalogue; *Looking At America*, Addison Gallery of American Art, Phillips Academy, Andover, Massachusetts.

1980: *Photographie als Kunst: Kunst als Photographie*, Museum Moderner Kunst, Vienna, catalogue; *Arte Americana Contemporanea*, Civici Musei e Gallerie Di Storia e Arte, Udine, Italy, catalogue; *A Sense of Place: The American Landscape in Recent Art*, University Gallery, University of Massachusetts, Amherst, catalogue; *Amalgam*, Castelli Graphics, New York; *Aspects of the 1970's*, DeCordova Museum, Lincoln, Massachusetts.

1979: *Venturi and Rausch Architecture*, Kunstgewerbermuseum, Zurich; *Industrial Sights*, Whitney Museum of American Art, Downtown Branch, New York; *Lewis Baltz, Mark Cohen, Eve Sonneman*, Moderna Museet, Stockholm, circulating; *American Images*, The Corcoran Gallery of Art, Washington, D.C., circulating, catalogue.

1978: *Architectures*, Bibliothèque Nationale, Paris; *Mirrors and Windows: American Photography Since 1960*, The Museum of Modern Art, New York, circulating, catalogue; *The Photograph As Artifice*, California State University, Long Beach, catalogue; *23 Photographers: 23 Directions*, Walker Art Gallery, Liverpool, England, catalogue; *Certain Landscapes*, Castelli Graphics, New York; *Additional Information*, University of Maryland, College Park; *Baltz, Deal, Gohlke, Shore*, Werkstatt für Photographie, Berlin; *Changing Prospects*, The National Gallery of Canada, Ottawa, catalogue; *Facades*, Hayden Art Gallery, Massachusetts Institute of Technology, Cambridge.

1977: *Biennial Exhibition*, Whitney Museum of American Art, New York; *La Photographie creative au XXe Siecle*, Musée National d'Art Moderne, Centre Pompidou, Paris, catalogue; *Art and Architecture*, Galerie Magers, Bonn, catalogue; *American Photographers*, Galerie im Taxispalais, Innsbruck and Museum des XX Jahrhunderts, Vienna, catalogue; *Master Photographs from Toronto Collections*, York University Art Gallery, Toronto, catalogue.

1976: *IXe Biennale de Paris à Nice*, La Galerie de les Ponchettes et de la Galerie Marine, Nice, catalogue; *Photography For Collectors*, The Museum of Modern Art, New York; *Contemporary American Photography*, Edinburgh Art Festival; *Project Rebuild*, Grey Art Gallery and Study Center, New York University; *America As Art*, National Museum of American Art, Washington, D.C.

1975: *IXe Biennale de Paris*, Musée d'Art Moderne de la Ville de Paris, catalogue; *New Topographics*, International Museum of Photography at George Eastman House, Rochester, New York, Otis Art Institute of Parsons School of Design, Los Angeles, and the The Art Museum, Princeton University, New Jersey, catalogue; *14 American Photographers*, The Baltimore Museum of Art, Maryland, circulating, catalogue.

1974: *Photography Unlimited*, Fogg Art Museum, Harvard University, Cambridge, Massachusetts; *Art Now '74*, Kennedy Center for the Performing Arts, Washington, D.C., catalogue.

1973: *Two Americans*, Musée d'Art Moderne de la Ville de Paris; *Contemporary Documents*, School of Art and Architecture, Yale University, New Haven, Connecticut; *Recent Acquisitions*, The Museum of Modern Art, New York; *24 from LA*, San Francisco Museum of Modern Art.

1971: *The Crowded Vacancy: Three Los Angeles Photographers*, Memorial Union Art Gallery, University of California, Davis, Pasadena Museum of Modern Art, California, and the San Francisco Museum of Modern Art, catalogue.

Selected Bibliography

Baltz, Lewis. "Book Reviews: The New West," *Art in America,* March-April, 1975

    ed. *Contemporary American Photographic Works,* Museum of Fine Arts, Houston, Texas, 1977

    Photographie aus Berlin, with John Gossage, Castelli Graphics, New York, 1984

    "Konsumerterror," *Aperture,* Fall 1984

    "Landscape Problems: Edward Weston, California Landscapes," *Aperture,* Spring 1985

    "Too Old To Rock, Too Young To Die," *American Images,* Viking Press, New York, 1985

    "Notizen zu Waffenruhe," *Camera Austria,* June 1988

    "The Raft of the Medusa," *Revue Française d'Etudes Americaines,* February 1989

    "In un Passagio Provisorio," *L'Unita,* August 23, 1989

Bourdier, Noel. "Sixièmes Rencontrés photographiques," *Artpress,* December 1987

Bowles, Demetra, ed. *Architype,* Spring 1981

Cuvelier, Pascaline. "Le depotoir de Baltz," *Liberation,* November 26, 1988

Davis, Douglas. "Art," *Newsweek,* December 8, 1975

    "Photography: California By Strobe Light," *Newsweek,* March 5, 1984

Decter, Joshua. "New York Reviews," *Arts Magazine,* December 1989

Durand, Regis. "Lewis Baltz, la mémoire mutilée des choses," *Artpress,* June 1986

    Le Regard Pensif, Éditions littéraires et artistiques/La Différence, Paris, 1988

Eveno, Claude, editor. *Cahiers du C.C.I.,* Musée National d'Art Moderne, Centre Pompidou, June 1986

Extra, July 1975

Fisher, Hal. "Reviews: San Francisco," *Artforum,* Summer 1984

Foster, Hal. "Reviews: New York," *Artforum,* May 1980

Foote, Nancy. "The Anti-Photographers," *Artforum,* September 1976

Fornio, Giorgio and Silvana Turzio. "L'occhio sul mirino: Lewis Baltz", *L'Arca,* February 1989

George, Phillip. "New Topographics," *The Guardian,* September 23, 1981

Grundberg, Andy. "Book Reviews: Park City," *Art in America,* May 1981

    "Photography Books," *New York Times Book Review,* December 7, 1986

Guibert, Herve. "Des photographes et des murs," *Le Monde,* May 7, 1978

Hagan, Charles. "Reviews: New York," *Artforum,* November 1989

Haworth-Booth, Mark. "London: American Photography," *Burlington Magazine,* August 1985

Kardon, Janet. *Lewis Baltz Photographs, 1967-1975,* Philadelphia College of Art, Pennsylvania, 1975

Lamarche-Vadel, Bernard. "Lewis Baltz: San Quentin Point," *Cardinaux,* Fall 1986

Mutti, Roberto. "Obievitivo Sul Nostro Habitat," *La Republica,* October 5, 1989

Lemagny, Jean-Claude and Andre Rouille. *Histoire de la Photographie,* Bordos S.A., Paris, 1986

Levin, Eric. "Picks and Pans: Books: San Quentin Point," *People,* February 9, 1987

Marincola, Paula. "Skeptical Resort," *Afterimage,* November 4, 1981

Pittolo, Veronique. "L'image en chantier," *Le Figaro,* October 27, 1988

Plagens, Peter. "Los Angeles," *Artforum,* October 1971

Rogiers, Patrick. "De l'amour de la nature à la perception de l'étrange," *Le Monde,* October 1, 1986

Sekula, Allen. "Dismantling Modernism," and "School Is a Factory," in *Photography Against the Grain,* Nova Scotia College of Art and Design Press, Halifax, 1985

Turner, Peter. *The History of Photography,* Bison Books, London, 1987

Westerbeck, Colin. "Photography Now," *Artforum,* January 1979

Selected Public Collections

Addison Gallery of American Art, Phillps Academy, Andover, Massachusetts; Art Gallery of Ontario, Toronto, Canada; The Art Institute of Chicago; The Art Museum, Princeton University, New Jersey; Australian National Gallery, Canberra; The Baltimore Museum of Art, Maryland; Bibliothèque Nationale, Paris; The Brooklyn Museum, New York; Cincinnati Art Museum, Ohio; The Corcoran Gallery of Art, Washington, D.C.; Dallas Museum of Art, Texas; Des Moines Art Center, Iowa; Fogg Art Museum, Harvard University, Cambridge, Massachusetts; Fond National d'Art Contemporain, Paris; Fonds Régional d'Art Contemporain Bretagne, Chateaugiron, France; Henie-Onstad Art Center, Oslo; High Museum of Art, Atlanta, Georgia; International Center of Photography, New York; International Museum of Photography at George Eastman House, Rochester, New York; Kawasaki City Museum, Japan; Los Angeles County Museum of Art; The Metropolitan Museum of Art, New York; Milwaukee Art Museum, Wisconsin; The Minneapolis Institute of Art, Minnesota; Moderna Museet, Stockholm; Museo Civico e Gallerie d'Arte, Udine, Italy; Museum of Contemporary Art, Los Angeles, California; Museum of Fine Arts, Boston, Massachusetts; Museum of Fine Arts, Houston, Texas; Museum of Modern Art, New York; National Gallery of Canada, Ottawa; National Museum of American Art, Washington, D.C.; National Museum of Modern Art, Kyoto; Neuberger Museum, State University of New York, Purchase; Newport Harbor Art Museum, California; Oakland Museum, California; Palazzo Fortuny, Museo e Centro de Documentazione Fotografica, Venice; Philadelphia Museum of Art, Pennsylvania; The Power Gallery of Contemporary Art, University of Sydney, Australia; John and Mable Ringling Museum of Art, Sarasota, Florida; San Francisco Museum of Modern Art; Tokyo Institute of Polytechnics; University Art Museum, University of California, Berkeley; University Gallery, University of Massachusetts, Amherst; Victoria and Albert Museum, London; The Wellesley College Museum, Massachusetts; Frederick S. Wight Art Gallery, University of California, Los Angeles; Williams College Museum of Art, Williamstown, Massachusetts.

Contributors

Mowry Baden is a sculptor and Professor of Art, University of Victoria, British Columbia.

Olivier Boissiére is an architecture critic whose articles have appeared in *L'Arca, Architecture Aujourd'hui, Le Monde,* and was formerly the critic for *Le Matin.* Author of *Gehry, Site, Tigerman* (1980), *Streamline* (1987), "New York Viewed From the Sky," *Doublepage* (1989), as well as monographs on the work of Frank Gehry, Jean Nouvel and other interesting contemporary architects.

Gus Blaisdell lives in New Mexico. Film and art critic, poet, author, Adjunct Professor in Cinema Studies, University of New Mexico, Albuquerque. Co-author, with Lewis Baltz, of *Park City,* and Contributing Editor of *Artspace.*

Paolo Costantini lives in Venice and is Professor of Art History at the University of Architecture, Venice, Italy. Adjunct Curator, Palazzo Fortuny, Museo e Centro de Documentazione Fotografica, Venice. Author of *Nuovo Passagio Americano: Dialectical Landscapes,* and *L'insistenza dello squardo: Fotografie Italiano, 1839-1989,* with Italo Zannier, and Contributing Editor of *Fotologia.*

Mark Haworth-Booth is Assistant Keeper of the Department of Prints, Drawings, and Photographs at the Victoria and Albert Museum, London. He has written introductions to Bill Brandt's *London in the Thirties* (1984) and *Bill Brandt: Behind the Camera* (1985). He has edited and introduced *The Golden Age of British Photography, 1839-1900,* and more recently the exhibition and book *Photography Now.*

Marvin Heiferman lives in New York and was former Director, Castelli Photographs, New York. Co-curator, with Lisa Phillips, of *Image World,* Whitney Museum of American Art, New York, 1989; co-author, with Diane Keaton, of *Still Life,* (1983), and, with Carole Kismaric, of *I'm So Happy* (1990).

Shirley Irons is a painter who lives in New York. She writes informed consents for schizophrenics for a research group at N.Y.U. Medical Center, has published an article on gangliosides in *Psychopharmacology Bulletin,* was a co-editor of *Heresies, #20* on political activism, and has written about her painting for *BOMB* magazine. She is a founding member of GAG. She grew up in Staten Island and has paid attention to detritus all her life.

Jeff Kelley is a frequent contributor to *Artforum.*

Bernard Lamarche-Vadel lives in Brittany and Paris, France. His books include *Michel Ange* (1981), *Giacometti* (1985), *Joseph Beuys* (1985), *Keichi Tehara* (1986), and *Arman* (1988). He was founder of the magazines *Artists* (1979-82) and *Cardinaux* (1986-87). He has organized over fifty exhibitions of painting, sculpture, and photography in France and Europe.

Jane Livingston is the former Chief Curator and Associate Director of The Corcoran Gallery of American Art, Washington, D.C., 1975-89. Co-author, with Marcia Tucker, of *Bruce Nauman: Work From 1965 to 1972;* author of *Manuel Alvarez Bravo* (1976) and *Black Folk Art in America* (1982); co-author, with Rosalind Krauss, of *L'Amour fou: Photography and Surrealism* (1985); author of *Hispanic Art In The United States* (1987), *Lee Miller, Photographer* (1989) and *The New York School: Photography 1936-1963,* scheduled for 1992.

Michael Schmidt, photographer, lives in Berlin. Author of several monographs, including *Berlin/ Kruetzberg, Stadtbilder (1984)* and, with Einar Schlieff, *Waffenruhe (1987).*

Dedication

This book is dedicated to three women of great consequence in my life: to my daughter, Monica Baltz; to the memory of my friend, Toiny Castelli; and to Julia Brown Turrell, without whose courage and support this book and exhibition would not exist.   *Lewis Baltz*

Acknowledgments

There are a number of persons whose names are not mentioned elsewhere in this book whose assistance the artist and the Des Moines Art Center acknowledges gratefully. In Des Moines: the Board of Trustees, Julia Brown Turrell, M. Jessica Rowe, Susan Burgess, Sheryl L. West, Deborah Leveton, Connie Tartt Granberg, Robert C. Fuller, Penelepe C. Hunt, Joanie Kiernan, Patricia Baldwin, Wayne Masterson, Michael J. Willoughby, Alan L. Wise, and Margaret A. Willard, of the Des Moines Art Center; Tom Holtz, Connie Wilson, Nina Fowler, and Sharon Soder, of HoltzWilson Design Corporation. In New York: Mr. Leo Castelli, Ms. Pat Caporaso, Ms. Carrie Kahn, Ms. Hope Kaufman, Ms. Laura Moss, Ms. Jodi Sherer, Mr. Patrick Callery, Mr. Gary Graves, Mr. John Roche, of Castelli Graphics; Ms. Alanna Heiss, Ms. Rebecca Quaytman, Mr. Hank Stahler, and Mr. Tim Noe, of the Institute for Contemporary Art, P.S. 1 Museum; Mr. Renato Danese; Mr. Charles Miers; Mr. Robert Monk; Mr. Arthur Solway. In Washington, D.C.: Mr. John Gossage. In Florida: Mr. Timothy Eaton and Ms. Mary Anna Shoen, Boca Raton; Ms. Ileen Sheppard, of the John and Mable Ringling Museum of Art, Sarasota. In San Francisco: Suzann Dunaway, and Timothy Mosman, of Mills College Art Gallery, Oakland; Ms. Stephanie Cannizzo, of the University Art Museum, University of California, Berkeley; John Randolph and Bruce Tomb, Interim Office of Architects; Page Imageworks; and Ms. Catherine Wagner. In Los Angeles: Ms. Sheryl Conkleton and Mr. Robert Sobieszek, of the Los Angeles County Museum of Art; Mr. Frank Green; Ms. Theresa Luisotti, Mr. Mark Greenberg, and Ms. Nicole Greenberg; Mr. Paul Schimmel, of the Museum of Contemporary Art, Los Angeles; Mr. John Upton; and Mr. David Gardner, Gardner Lithograph. In Flagstaff, Arizona: Mr. James Turrell. In Albuquerque: Ms. Beth Hadas and Ms. Dana Asbury, of the University of New Mexico Press. In Paris: Mme. Michèle Chomette, Galerie Michèle Chomette; M. Regis Durand; M. François Hers. In London: Mr. Mark Holborn; Mrs. Cecil and Mr. Roger Jospe; and Mr. Peter Turner. In Essen, Germany: Ms. Ute Eskildsen. With special thanks to Mr. Marvin Heiferman and Ms. Carole Kismaric.

One of my best experiences in this project has been working with Connie Wilson, as she invented a new form for the "retrospective" book. Her vision and integrity—her refusal to rely on existing design strategies—showed me a new set of possibilities for book design and gave me a fresh perspective on my own work.   *Lewis Baltz*

Lewis Baltz: Rule Without Exception was organized by Julia Brown Turrell for the Des Moines Art Center, Iowa, and made possible through the support of: The Robert Mapplethorpe Foundation, Inc., New York; The Andy Warhol Foundation for the Visual Arts, Inc., New York; The National Endowment for the Arts, Washington, D.C.; The Jacqueline and Myron Blank Exhibition Fund, Des Moines; The Melva and Martin Bucksbaum Director's Discretionary Fund for Acquisition and Innovation, Des Moines; Kay and Matthew Bucksbaum, Des Moines; Theresa Luisotti, Office and Gallery RAM, Los Angeles and Tokyo; Stuart and Jane Zehngut, L.A. Art Exchange, Santa Monica; Dr. Mathew Naythons, Sausalito and New York; and John Upton, San Clemente. We gratefully acknowledge and appreciate their support.

"If we consider Jacques Derrida's analysis in this context we come across an answer which, to some extent, could only be derived from its extension. Lord Byron had provided the motif in his Don Juan, finished in 1824, that the end of the world was no longer nigh—it had actually long begun in the form of an internal death caused by coldness.

If our day and age, as Derrida thinks, can thus be considered postapocalyptic because the apocalypse—even the atomic one—has already taken place in thousandfold form in the media, and because there is no veritable apocalypse left to come, especially as there would be no audience for it anyway, then these findings do not yet provide an answer to the question concerning the reasons for this desire for apocalypse.

Far from any causal determination it can, nevertheless be said that an implication—if not an actual sense—of this kind of "...apocalysia...lies in the prevention of a real end of the world, or to put it bluntly, nobody is really frightened that the world is coming to an end, but a life without anxiety is much too dangerous...."

Dieter Lenzen
Disappearing Adulthood